STORY MADE SIMPLE

A NO-NONSENSE GUIDE TO THE ESSENTIAL ELEMENTS OF STORYTELLING

BRANDON MCNULTY

MIDNIGHT
POINT
PRESS

For my first creative writing teacher,
Mrs. Yonkoski

CONTENTS

INTRODUCTION

GET READY TO WRITE BETTER STORIES

Storytelling has one nightmare of a learning curve. Not only is it endless and arduous—half the battle is figuring out what you need to learn in the first place. Sure, plenty of guidebooks, online courses, and workshops offer direction, but the reality is that most writers feel completely lost from the get-go. Worse yet, due to a poor understanding of the craft, they often waste hundreds or even thousands of hours writing broken stories.

How do I know? I lived this nightmare.

Prior to independently publishing my novels and starting a YouTube writing channel, I made every mistake a fiction writer could make: one-dimensional characters, empty themes, aimless plot lines—you name it. There's no shame in making such mistakes and learning from them—that's part of the growth process—but I didn't know *what* I needed to learn. Unfortunately, that caused me to waste countless hours writing stories that went nowhere.

Which brings us to *Story Made Simple*. It's the book I wish someone had handed me when I was a twenty-year-old kid hungry to write something special. My goal here is to demystify the key elements of storytelling for new and veteran writers alike. Advice like this could've set me on the fast track and spared me from typing up nearly a dozen hideous, unreadable manuscripts.

Each of this book's eight chapters explores a specific element and offers insights, analysis, and "Action Step" sections that provide hands-on strategies for integrating these lessons into your writing. Everything is delivered with my no-nonsense style that YouTube audiences have appreciated for years, and throughout the book I include plenty of examples selected from popular movies and TV shows, though the lessons apply across all storytelling mediums.

Before we dig in, here's a brief overview of the eight elements:

- **Concept** is the central idea or selling point that serves as the story's blueprint.
- **Character** is the heart of a story—the fictional people who face conflict, make decisions, and embark on meaningful journeys.
- **Worldbuilding,** much more than a setting backdrop, impacts the characters and can itself behave like a character.
- **Theme** makes a story relevant to real life. Though often thought of as a message, theme runs deeper and binds every story element together.
- **Plot** is what happens on the surface—but that doesn't mean it's shallow. Plot serves as an external representation of a character's inner journey.
- **Story Structure** is the skeleton that supports the overall story. Many writers believe structure suppresses creativity, but that's false. Rather, structure *enables* creativity by providing a stable launching point for fresh ideas.

- **Scenes** are the building blocks of a story. They create change to drive the story forward.
- Finally, **Pacing** is the story's rhythm, which uses timing and emotion to keep an audience engaged.

You'll notice these elements overlap and influence each other. It's impossible to isolate each; Chapter 2 covers characters, but lessons on writing fictional people won't stop there. As we examine worldbuilding, theme, etc., we'll continue learning about characters—and other elements. This book aims to not only simplify storytelling but explore the craft from different angles to help you generate ideas.

With that said, let's get our creativity flowing by tackling the first element: concept.

CHAPTER 1
CONCEPT

STORYTELLING BEGINS WITH A CONCEPT, the foundational idea. The selling point. The blueprint for the narrative we're constructing. A good concept combines multiple ideas into a meaningful story full of possibilities. Whether the concept is as basic as "detectives solving murders" or as imaginative as "scientists visiting a theme park filled with cloned dinosaurs," it should inspire us to write.

This chapter will focus on building a strong concept. We'll discuss how to harvest worthwhile ideas, how to shape those ideas into an original blueprint, and how to further distinguish the concept with stylistic tools.

GETTING THE RIGHT IDEAS

There's no magic formula for identifying a great story idea. Most writers gather ideas in one of three ways: observation, inspiration, or experimentation.

Observation is pretty straightforward—simply live life and pay attention. If we notice something intriguing—perhaps an unusual image, person, or situation—we write about it. Imagine spotting a parked car with a big red "X" painted across the windshield. Maybe it leads to a story about how the "X" got there or one that proposes that anything painted with a red "X" is marked for a sinister ritual.

Then there's **inspiration**. Sometimes we enjoy a great book or movie and borrow an idea from it. Other inspiration may come from random thoughts. Or conversations. Or life experiences. When inspiration hits us, ideas pour out, and from there it's a matter of embracing the writing process.

Finally comes **experimentation**. This requires us to tinker with our ideas until we discover story material. It might sound like work, but we can take fun approaches. For example, author Ray Bradbury jotted down a list of things that scared him, and each day he wrote a short story about one of them. Bradbury ended up writing many iconic horror stories, and embracing his fears allowed him to be prolific.

CRAFTING AN ORIGINAL CONCEPT

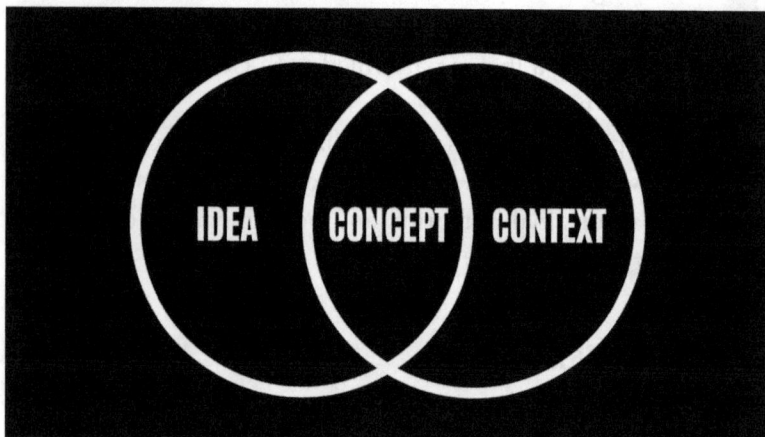

IDEA | CONCEPT | CONTEXT

If you've ever assembled furniture, a computer, or a treehouse, you know that having a list of parts isn't enough to complete the job. We also need directions, a basic plan for combining those parts into a greater whole.

Likewise, a list of story ideas won't assemble a story. Ideas are merely building blocks. If we aim to write engaging fiction, we must craft an original concept that establishes a blueprint for storytelling. We do this by combining two (or more) ideas. Relax —they don't have to be brilliant ideas. Just take familiar ones and mix them together in a fresh, unexpected way.

For example, back in the 1990s there was an obscure little movie called *The Lion King*. It placed the familiar idea of *Hamlet* within a fresh context, the animal kingdom. Classic Shakespearean Idea + Fresh Fantasy Context = Originality.

Another example is *Jurassic Park*. The movie placed the fresh concept of cloning dinosaurs in the familiar context of a horror story—specifically a haunted house tale in which a sin is committed and monsters punish those responsible. Fresh Sci-Fi Idea + Classic Haunted House Context = Originality.

Finally, in the TV series *Dexter*, a serial killer who exclusively kills bad guys works for the police. Fresh Serial Killer Idea + Classic Crime Drama Context = Originality.

Experimenting with various ideas can generate original concepts and energize the writing process. When two unrelated ideas collide, they demand to be explored. Then it's up to the writer to keep the momentum rolling.

You might be wondering…is originality completely necessary? What if we *can't* come up with an original concept? Are we doomed to write something boring and forgettable?

Not at all. Certain stories rely more on execution than concept, and there's no shame in writing something familiar. Some audiences love stories that deliver familiar ideas in a familiar context. Hallmark has a channel devoted to such movies. They're not groundbreaking, but they give audiences what they want. Another example is the 2013 movie *The Conjuring*, which is about paranormal investigators who investigate a haunted house. It's a basic concept, yet audiences flocked to see it in theaters because of its old-school stylistic approach.

We'll talk more about style later in this chapter. For now, let's tackle our first set of Action Steps.

ACTION STEPS: BUILDING AN ORIGINAL CONCEPT

STEP #1: Gather ideas and contexts through observation, inspiration, or experimentation

Try these three methods for locating ideas and contexts and see if one works for you.

First, observe the world around you. Pay attention to interesting people, objects, or locations. If you spot a jogger wearing only one shoe, ask yourself, how did they lose the other? If you see a baby carriage floating in your neighbor's swimming pool, ask yourself, how did it get there? If you drive past an abandoned building with busted windows, think about how the windows got busted or who might be squatting inside.

Next, add a dash of inspiration and then absorb stories and life itself. Pay attention to things that excite you. If you just watched a mind-blowing heist movie, create a heist scenario of your own. If you love reading about post-war Japan, set a story there. If you've been working at a hospital for five years, consider writing about daily life in the ICU.

Finally, welcome experimentation. Jot down recent thoughts, experiences, or emotions. If you're planning a Christmas party, consider writing about how people will celebrate Christmas one hundred years from now. If you've been feeling angry, write about how an angry character solves their problems. Or drop the angry character into your distant-future Christmas party and see what happens.

STEP #2: Merge the familiar with the fresh

You've gathered ideas and contexts. Now start mixing them together until something unique emerges. First, draw a line down the middle of a sheet of paper. List ideas in one column and contexts in the other. Then draw lines connecting the entries. See if anything unexpected arises and inspires you.

Another strategy is to combine opposites to reveal fresh possibilities. If you're eager to write about revenge, place revenge in the unexpected context of an Easter egg hunt or a petting zoo or another setting that isn't typically associated with vengeance.

STEP #3: Connect your concept to other story elements

The other elements will become clearer as we continue through this book, but for now think about how your central idea can link to characters, worldbuilding, themes, plot lines, etc.

For instance, you might explore a concept about a family trying to escape a monster. Character and plot are already baked in, but go deeper. Add some worldbuilding: "A family escapes monsters in a post-apocalyptic world where making noise leads to instant death." That's the premise of the 2018 movie *A Quiet Place*. Worldbuilding elevates it from a basic monster movie to a memorable one.

STYLE: PERSONALIZING A CONCEPT

When it comes to crafting a concept, ideas are critical, but so is the stylistic approach we take.

Personal style determines how we uniquely express ideas. It's the fingerprint that distinguishes our work. It's who we are on the written page.

The writing process is essentially a series of creative choices, and style determines each choice, whether it's the characters we include, the themes we explore, or the pacing rhythms we set. We'll discuss these elements in detail over the next seven chapters, but now let's focus on two stylistic components that impact a story's concept: tone and mood.

TONE: THE STORY'S ATTITUDE

Tone is the attitude the writer assumes toward the story. A well-chosen tone adds flavor to the narrative while also setting expectations for how audiences should respond to the subject matter. Any subject can be approached with a variety of tones. For example, look at Batman. The classic 1960s *Batman* TV show adopts a campy tone that encourages audiences to have some laughs. By comparison, the severe tone of the 2022 movie *The Batman* puts audiences on alert from the get-go.

When crafting a concept, it's important to consider tone, as tone determines how we build from the concept. In most cases, tone fits into one of two basic categories: serious or lighthearted. When writers adopt a serious tone, audiences worry when characters face conflict. A lighthearted tone invites audiences to smile (or maybe laugh) when characters struggle.

Unsure whether to commit to a serious or lighthearted tone? Don't worry. Tone doesn't have to be consistent. Just because we want to tell a serious story doesn't mean every single scene has to be as serious as family court. There's always room for flexibility.

When it comes to shifting between tones, first **we need to respect our story, characters, and audience**. Our goal is to captivate audiences by taking them on a meaningful journey. Meaning arises from sincere moments, so we need to identify scenes that need to be serious, especially scenes that include danger, tragedy, and major character growth. These should be played straight. We don't want to undercut a sincere moment with silly descriptions, goofy dialogue, or slapstick humor—unless we're writing a ridiculously over-the-top comedy.

From there, target low-energy scenes that might benefit from lighthearted fun. Switching to a comedic tone during an info dump can spice up an otherwise boring section. We can also use well-timed humor during prolonged action sequences, such as when Legolas and Gimli crack jokes during battle in the *Lord of the Rings* movies. Though the battles themselves are serious, the tone shifts during low moments and provides a welcome breather from the tension.

The movie *Die Hard* does an excellent job of shifting between tones. It takes itself seriously with high-stakes drama while also integrating dark comedy at opportune times. For example, compare the deaths of company president Joe Takagi and the obnoxious yuppie Harry Ellis. Takagi is portrayed as a respectable leader, and when the terrorists shoot him, his murder serves as a tragic moment that raises the stakes. Later, after helping the terrorists, Ellis is killed in similar fashion, and his death is portrayed as darkly comedic—the villain even smirks before shooting him. Two deaths, two different tones, yet each works because the tone satisfies the audience's expectations.

MOOD: THE STORY'S EMOTIONAL VIBE

Tone and mood are often mistaken for the same thing. While there is overlap, they are separate animals. Tone, as we established, is the writer's attitude toward the work. **Mood** is the emotional vibe the work evokes, and it constantly shifts from situation to situation. In fact, we might describe a story as a series of changing moods.

It might help to think of mood as an emotional roller coaster that barrels through highs and lows. When constructing our coaster, we shift between positive and negative emotions. For example, if a bride is kidnapped en route to her wedding, hope shifts to despair. If a detective finds a clue leading to the kidnapper, despair shifts to renewed hope. But if the groom murders the detective, renewed hope shifts to even greater despair.

To better understand the difference between tone and mood, consider the prologue from the 2001 film adaptation of *Lord of the Rings: The Fellowship of the Ring*. The prologue invokes a sincere tone while it establishes the history of Middle Earth. Though the tone remains consistent throughout the prologue, the audience experiences multiple emotional shifts. Initially, a voiceover creates an ominous atmosphere, explaining that "The world has changed" and "Much that once was, is lost." Desperation follows as Elves and Men battle Sauron's forces; the situation appears hopeless. Then Isildur defeats Sauron and claims the Ring, creating a sense of relief. However, that relief is short lived; Isildur surrenders to the Ring's power, and the prologue ends on a note of despair.

When crafting our concept, it's important to consider mood. Stories can teach lessons or inspire or break hearts, but only if we deliver compelling emotional experiences. As writers, it's our job to be emotional drug dealers, and we need to examine our concept and determine what moods it can evoke.

ACTION STEPS: SETTING THE TONE AND MOOD

STEP #1: Determine the overall tone

A story can be as severe as *Schindler's List* or as ridiculous as *Airplane!* Most fall somewhere in the middle. When crafting your concept, consider your overall tone. Be aware of it. Mark it down. Then make a plan to establish that tone early.

If you're aiming for a predominantly serious tone, open with serious events. If you prefer to be lighthearted, adopt a comedic attitude while introducing characters. And if you expect to frequently bounce between tones, consider opening the story with one foot in serious territory and the other in lighthearted territory.

STEP #2: Brainstorm your story's emotional ups and downs

The mood will usually be established by how characters feel, so put your characters through both positive and negative experiences. If the focus is exclusively one way or the other, the story will get old fast. But if triumph leads to defeat and defeat leads to triumph, the emotional experience will be dynamic.

Though your characters will encounter many emotional shifts throughout the writing process, it's never too early to think about the overall trajectory of their journey and which moments will have the greatest impact.

Without overthinking, jot down ten positive things that might happen to your character and ten negative things. See if any of these events connect. If they do, congratulations—you've taken the first step toward telling a meaningful, emotional story.

CHEAT SHEET

- Concept is the story's central idea or selling point, as well as the story's blueprint.
- Original concepts combine an idea and context in unexpected ways.
- Style is a writer's personal touch, which distinguishes and enhances the concept.
- Tone is the attitude the writer takes toward the narrative. It influences how the audience interprets characters and their struggles.
- Mood is the emotional vibe that the author evokes, and it changes from situation to situation.

CHAPTER 2
CHARACTER

WE ALL KNOW that great characters lead to great stories, but many of us struggle when creating imaginary people. Though we dream of populating our fiction with characters who feel realistic and alive, too often we pollute the written page with walking cliches.

But that's no big deal, right? After all, if our characters suck, we can always make up ground elsewhere by bolstering the other story elements...right?

Well, here's the bad news. Most audiences, whether they realize it or not, prioritize character above all else. This is because characters give a narrative its heart—its emotional charge. Personal struggles drum up meaning and intrigue. If we ignore character, our story devolves into a sequence of cold, empty events.

Obviously, we want stories that pop and sizzle, so this chapter will focus on delivering dynamic, memorable characters. Specifically, we'll focus on selecting the right cast, creating characters who engage on multiple levels, and laying the groundwork for compelling transformation arcs.

THE IMPORTANCE OF CHARACTER ROLES

Before delving into what makes characters dynamic, we need to discuss the five basic character roles. These determine each character's level of significance, depth, and screen time. More importantly, these roles indicate how characters should function within the plot.

PROTAGONISTS

The protagonist is the main character. Though often labeled as the "hero," not all protagonists are morally good like Spider-Man or Ellen Ripley from *Alien*. Darker, less moral characters like Walter White from *Breaking Bad* or Michael Corleone from *The Godfather* also serve as protagonists, despite lacking traditionally heroic qualities.

The protagonist is typically the character with the most capacity for growth or the most capacity to effect change. For example, in *Star Wars* Luke Skywalker, Princess Leia, and Obi-Wan Kenobi all share the same goal: defeating the Empire. But Luke best fits the protagonist role because of his lack of Jedi training, which lays the foundation for strong character growth.

That said, protagonists don't necessarily have to grow. In *Law & Order* the protagonists seek justice in each episode, but rarely do they undergo meaningful transformations. Instead, they add personality and humanity to the story while attempting to effect change in their world.

ANTAGONISTS

The antagonist directly opposes the protagonist. Commonly referred to as "villains," antagonists may or may not be villainous. The Joker in *The Dark Knight* is certainly villainous. He robs banks, blows up hospitals, and murders people—including his own henchmen. On the other hand, Apollo Creed from the *Rocky* movies is not villainous. Apollo is the heavyweight boxing champion who opposes the protagonist, but Apollo never does anything immoral or disgusting.

Antagonists light the spark that ignites the main conflict. They want something, they pursue it, and their actions force the protagonist to react. This is most obvious in mysteries where the antagonist commits murder and forces a detective to solve the crime. Same idea applies to action-adventure stories in which an antagonist pursues world domination and thereby forces the protagonist to intervene.

Once a story's main conflict is established, the antagonist continues to pursue their goal while battling the protagonist. Both sides then act and react until their final confrontation determines the outcome of the story.

Major Supporting Characters

These are key players who orbit the protagonist or antagonist. Common types include sidekicks, allies, rivals, mentors, romantic partners, and family members. These characters not only influence plot events but also challenge the protagonist to rethink personal beliefs and thereby grow.

Side characters play a critical role in subplots. **Subplots** (which we'll discuss in Chapter 5) are secondary storylines that enhance our understanding of characters, themes, and events. Romantic subplots are popular because the romantic partner typically represents a lesson the protagonist must learn. For example, *Raiders of the Lost Ark* has a romantic subplot involving

Indiana Jones and his ex-girlfriend Marion. Early on, we learn that their prior relationship crumbled because Indy valued ancient treasures over her. Throughout *Raiders*, Indy continues to chase ancient artifacts before finally recognizing Marion's love as his true treasure.

MINOR CHARACTERS

While major supporting characters play relatively crucial roles, minor characters have less impact. They might have names, personalities, and backstories, but we won't see them undergoing character development or challenging the hero to transform. Instead, a minor character might show up temporarily to help advance the plot, create obstacles, deepen the worldbuilding, or provide comic relief.

STOCK CHARACTERS

These unimportant, one-dimensional characters are meant to be forgettable. Stock characters exist to perform low-stakes tasks and populate the story world. If our villain takes a cab to the airport, the cab driver would be a stock character. Later, the flight attendant who escorts the villain to their seat is another stock character. Same with all the nameless passengers on the plane.

Newer writers often make the mistake of creating flashy stock characters who become distractions. For instance, if we meet a cab driver named Jeremiah Phonebooth who oozes personality and hints at having a colorful backstory, we'll expect him to reappear later. But if Mr. Phonebooth doesn't reappear, he'll feel like a loose end to the audience.

ACTION STEPS: CASTING CHARACTERS

STEP #1: Create your protagonist and antagonist at the same time

A story's main conflict arises when the protagonist and antagonist battle over the same goal. If you want a shortcut for creating these characters, think of them as two sides of the same coin. Often they have something in common: same career, same bloodline, same tragic backstory, etc. Figure out what they have in common, how their values differ, and why these two characters might fight over the same goal.

For example, in the 2002 movie *Spider-Man*, both Spider-Man and the Green Goblin are superpowered outlaws who hide their identities while impacting New York City. However, their values differ. Spider-Man responsibly uses his powers to protect the public while the Goblin uses his powers to seek revenge and carry out selfish goals.

STEP #2: Choose appropriate supporting characters

Major side characters should challenge the protagonist (or antagonist) in meaningful ways. The word "meaningful" is important here. When surveying your cast, ask yourself, "Does each side character create meaningful conflict that impacts the protagonist's journey?" We'll talk more about journeys and growth arcs later in this chapter, but for now, think about the relationship between your protagonist and side characters. Determine what lessons your protagonist might learn while interacting with the supporting cast.

STEP #3: Draw a Character Web

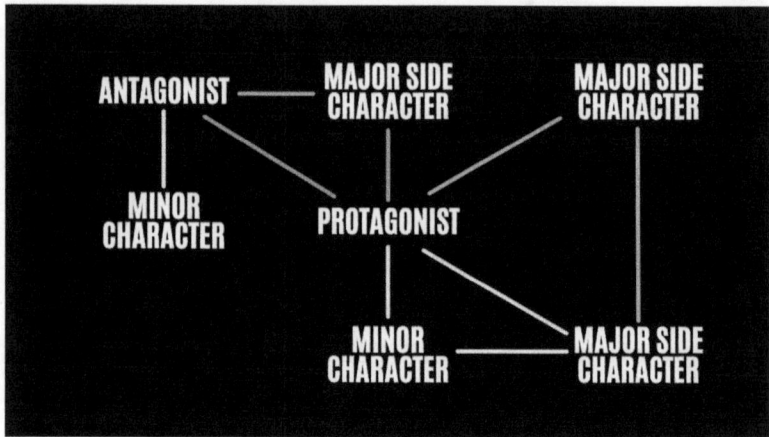

Here's a great strategy for organizing your main cast. First, write your protagonist's name in the center of a sheet of paper. Then surround it with the names of other important characters. At minimum include the protagonist, antagonist, and major supporting characters.

Next, draw lines connecting any two characters who have a personal bond. Friends, family, ex-lovers, coworkers, neighbors, rivals—if there's a relationship, draw a connecting line. Maybe even employ colored lines to represent positive, neutral, or hostile relationships.

During this exercise, you'll notice that some characters have more connections than others. For instance, your protagonist might be linked to most of the main cast, while a side character has only one meaningful connection. If that side character is meant to play a minor role, that's fine, but see if you can build other connections to create more complexity.

To be clear, the goal of this exercise isn't to link every single cast member. Rather, it's to give you a visual representation of how your characters relate to each other. Relationships add conflict and emotion to a story, so embrace opportunities to draw connections.

CRAFTING REALISTIC CHARACTERS

"Shallow."

"Cliched."

"One-dimensional."

No writer wants these criticisms directed at their major characters. And yet audiences deliver such complaints every day in blog posts, book reviews, and casual conversation. Their frustration arises not just because paper-thin characters provide little to chew on but because such characters also lead to boring, predictable narratives.

Thankfully, it doesn't take a miracle to solve this problem. If we want engaging stories, we need to create characters who are dynamic and multidimensional. That might sound challenging, but there's a simple four-step method for fleshing out characters.

LEVELS OF CHARACTER DEPTH

1. GOAL
2. MOTIVATION
3. CHARACTER LIE
4. TRAGIC BACKSTORY

The secret involves giving them meaningful goals and deep motivations.

A **story goal** is what a character wants—something tangible and achievable. For example, in the TV series *Breaking Bad*, Walter White wants to make money by cooking meth. He strives toward this goal, but that goal alone isn't enough to make him multidimensional. There must be a "why" behind it. In other words, he needs a compelling emotional reason—or **motivation** —for pursuing his goal.

Why does Walt want to cook meth? Because he possesses intense feelings of inferiority. After receiving a cancer diagnosis, he realizes he hasn't provided enough financial security for his family. That sense of powerlessness motivates him to cook meth —while also making him a dynamic protagonist.

Strong goals and motivations are a great start, but we can dig deeper to make characters even more realistic. In her popular blog, developmental editor Ellen Brock explains that there are two additional levels beneath motivation.

The third level is the **character lie**, which causes their motivation. The character harbors a twisted belief about themselves or the world around them, and this belief paints their world as a hostile environment. For example, Walter White believes the world owes him a debt because everyone has ignored his intelligence for so long.

The fourth level is the **tragic backstory**, which is a single tragic event or a pattern of tragedies that scar the character. For instance, Walter White once co-founded a tech company and sold his shares for $5,000. Later, the company's value skyrocketed to $2 billion while Walter scraped by as a high school teacher. This tragic backstory causes his character lie, which causes his motivation, which causes his story goal.

DO CHARACTERS NEED TO BE LIKABLE?

Some writing gurus insist characters must be likable. Others argue that characters should be relatable. While likability and relatability certainly score points with audiences, neither is mandatory. What truly matters is that characters are **engaging**.

To engage means to make the audience care about what happens—to build an emotional connection, whether positive or negative. Characters should grab our attention and hold it, regardless of whether we like or relate to them.

In his classic writing guide *The Techniques of the Selling Writer*, Dwight V. Swain says the secret to building emotionally engaging characters is making the audience feel sympathy, empathy, or envy.

Sympathy means giving us a reason to feel sorry for the character. Maybe they lose their job, their family, or a golden opportunity. Maybe they're trapped in a miserable marriage. Maybe they receive a terminal diagnosis. Maybe a Terminator is trying to kill them. There are countless possibilities, and if we create sympathy, our audience will root for characters to overcome their miserable situation.

Empathy means helping us understand a character. If we grasp their motivations, we can engage with them. For instance, in *The Godfather* Michael Corleone is introduced as a war hero who loves his family but refuses to participate in their organized crime business. Initially we understand Michael as a morally upright outsider; as the story develops, we continue to engage with him as he abandons his morals to protect his family.

Envy makes us wish we could step into a character's shoes. We envy characters who are skilled, confident, intelligent, attractive, wealthy, successful, admired, etc. Characters like Indiana Jones engage us because we want his fearless attitude, clever mind, and iconic bullwhip, among other things.

It's worth noting that we can combine all three emotions to build a compelling character. Batman has entertained audiences since the 1930s, and he's often portrayed as someone worthy of our sympathy, empathy, and envy. We sympathize with him when his parents are murdered, we empathize with him as he fights crime to avenge their deaths, and we envy his skills, strength, courage, wealth, and gadgets.

ACTION STEPS: CREATING REALISTIC AND ENGAGING CHARACTERS

STEP #1: Deepen your major characters

Once you've developed a general idea of your main cast, dig deeper, level by level, starting with their story goal. The goal itself doesn't need to be original—in fact, most characters have simple, straightforward goals like becoming king, winning a competition, or getting revenge.

From there, ask yourself, "Why does the character want their goal?" The *why* is their motivation, and it should add a unique flavor to their journey. Multiple characters may want to become king, but what differentiates them is *why* they want that goal. One may pursue kingship to wage war on foreign lands, another to satisfy his power-hungry ego, and another to fulfill his birthright. Test out different motivations and see what best fits your story.

Then consider the character's lie: "What harmful belief has corrupted the character's worldview?" Perhaps he believes the outside world presents a hostile threat, and that creates a need to conquer foreign lands, which motivates him to become king.

Finally, decide the tragic backstory. Ask yourself, "What past event created the character's twisted worldview?" Maybe at a young age his house was burned down by invaders, and that caused him to see the outside world as hostile.

STEP #2: Decide how to make major characters engaging

Sympathy is the fastest way to get the audience invested in a protagonist, so consider writing early scenes that involve your character suffering defeat, injury, or humiliation.

Next, look for opportunities to create empathy and help the audience understand who the character is, why they do what they do, and so on.

Finally, evoking envy can make a protagonist engaging, and it works especially well when introducing antagonists. Showcase their skills, intelligence, resources, and moral flexibility while they pursue a goal. Many audiences love the sense of catharsis that antagonists offer—we admire how they brazenly pursue their darkest desires without shame or hesitation.

CREATING CHANGE: CHARACTER ARCS, FLAWS, AND LIES

Once we've crafted a layered, engaging character, it's time to give them a compelling arc. A **character arc** is an up-and-down journey of transformation that occurs over the course of a story. In other words, the character changes for better or worse—or in some cases they may change *other people* for better or worse.

The easiest way to confirm whether a character transforms is by checking their status at the beginning and end of a story. Think of these as before-and-after snapshots. If the "before" snapshot reveals a miserable, unfulfilled loser and the "after" snapshot shows a confident champion, the character has completed an arc.

But remember, arcs don't happen instantly. Growth is a process, and it involves characters struggling with their flaws and lies.

FLAWS

A **character flaw** is a negative behavior that prevents someone from being happy, like selfishness, recklessness, cowardice, addiction, and greed. Flaws create conflict, make characters complex, and steer the plot in surprising directions as characters surrender to weaknesses.

The opposite of a flaw is a **strength**. In order to change for the better, a character begins with a flaw and grows toward a strength. Cowardice becomes bravery, addiction becomes sobriety, greed becomes charity, and so on. In the movie *Groundhog Day*, weatherman Phil Connors starts as a self-absorbed jerk and grows toward the strength of selflessness. This allows him to complete his arc and live a happy life.

LIES

Earlier in this chapter, we introduced the idea of a **character lie**, which is a negative, misguided belief a character holds about themselves or the world around them. Something like "I'm not worthy of love" or "Success is more important than friendship" or "People only respect you if you're wealthy." As previously discussed, the lie results from backstory events. One major event or a series of smaller events may hammer the lie into someone's brain.

A character who believes a lie will be miserable or unfulfilled until they embrace its opposite **truth**. So if the lie is that "Career success is more important than friendship," the truth would be "Friendship is more important than career success."

In *Harry Potter & the Sorcerer's Stone*, Harry believes he isn't special or worthy of love. That's his lie, which he believes because he's an orphan who was treated horribly by his aunt and uncle. Over time, however, he discovers that he *is* special, and he finds love by developing friendships with Ron and Hermione. Ultimately, Harry rejects the lie and accepts a new truth, which completes his arc and leads to happiness.

DIFFERENTIATING BETWEEN FLAWS AND LIES

Many writers find flaws and lies confusing because the two ideas are similar. Both create conflict, and they can work in tandem to make a character miserable. In fact, sometimes a flaw and lie overlap. In *Groundhog Day*, Phil Connors engages in self-centered behavior (which is his flaw) and he also believes he's better than everyone (which is a self-centered lie). We see a similar case in *Star Wars* with Han Solo. Han's flaw is that he's self-centered, and he believes the lie that there's no cause worth risking his life for. When he overcomes one, he overcomes both —although you can argue his flaw remains after the first movie.

Which brings up another key point: lies are typically conquered, while flaws may persist—especially in a trilogy or series. Harry Potter overcomes lies about his personal worth while still surrendering to his flaw of impulsiveness. That flaw keeps him realistic and relatable while he continues to grow by overcoming new lies.

THREE TYPES OF CHARACTER ARCS

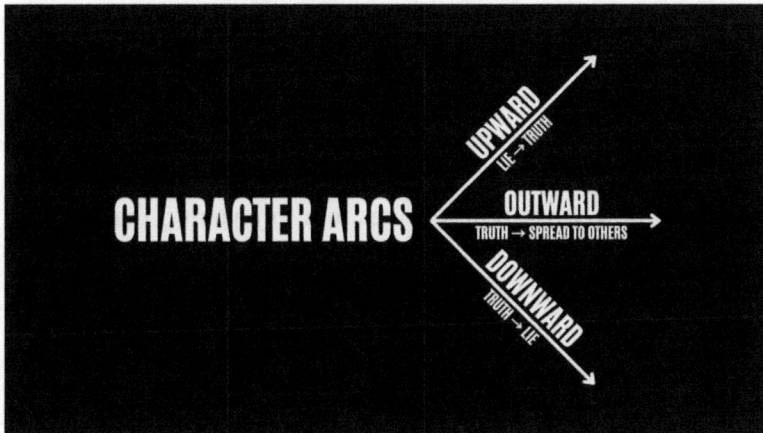

CHARACTER ARCS

UPWARD
LIE → TRUTH

OUTWARD
TRUTH → SPREAD TO OTHERS

DOWNWARD
TRUTH → LIE

Though character arcs are frequently associated with personal improvement, not all arcs end with someone changing for the better. There's room for variety, and the basic trajectory of a character arc can be upward, outward, or downward.

In the ubiquitous **Upward Arc,** a character believes a lie but grows to accept a truth. It's the arc Spider-Man undergoes in the 2002 movie. Throughout the story he faces a series of emotional ups and downs while wrestling with the lie that he doesn't need to be responsible. After recognizing the consequences of his reckless choices, he decides to embrace the truth that he must become responsible as he enters adulthood.

In the **Outward Arc,** a character believes a truth and attempts to teach it to others. Meanwhile, the character is challenged and even tempted by those who believe the lie. In *Star Wars: Return of the Jedi,* Luke believes that the peaceful, nonviolent way of the Jedi will bring order to the galaxy. Luke attempts to convince Darth Vader of this, but Vader repeatedly rejects the idea. Ultimately, Luke sticks to his Jedi beliefs, even in the face of death. This compels Vader to change, which completes Luke's Outward Arc (as well as Vader's Upward Arc).

In the **Downward Arc,** a character initially believes a truth but later embraces a lie. Author K.M. Weiland identifies other variations of this tragic arc in her book *Creating Character Arcs,* but for the sake of simplicity, we'll say a Downward Arc involves a shift from truth to lie. For example, in *The Godfather* Michael Corleone initially believes that living a moral life is more important than achieving power. However, Michael's desire to protect his family drives him to abandon that truth in favor of the lie that achieving power is more important. Ultimately, he becomes the ruthless head of a crime family, and his personal relationships suffer.

During the upcoming chapter on Story Structure we'll take a deeper dive into character arcs. We'll also look at these three examples in greater detail.

ACTION STEPS: CRAFTING A CHARACTER JOURNEY

STEP #1: Determine what type of arc your protagonist will undergo

If you want to save yourself time and headaches, decide early on whether you're working with an Upward, Outward, or Downward Arc. By determining the beginning and ending points of your protagonist's journey, you simplify the writing process and give yourself direction.

For instance, if you know your character will overcome their lie at the end, you also know there must be key moments of positive growth along the way. From there, it's a matter of sprinkling in those moments throughout the story.

STEP #2: Pick flaws and lies that intensify the character arc

To create strong internal conflict, give your protagonist a flaw or lie that creates compelling dilemmas. While you're at it, identify the flaw's opposite strength and the lie's opposite truth. Recognizing these will help you track your protagonist's growth over the course of the story.

If you're struggling to come up with a flaw or lie, figure out what your protagonist fears. Fear generates internal conflict and causes people to develop harmful habits, behaviors, and mindsets. For example, someone who fears failure might procrastinate at work, sabotage personal relationships, or hold a low opinion of themselves—all of which can create compelling drama while the character attempts to overcome their fear.

STEP #3: Plan for emotional ups and downs

Character arcs don't happen instantly. They unfold over time while your protagonist makes mistakes, faces consequences, and tests out both the lie and truth before making a definitive final choice.

To keep the journey suspenseful, include good and bad choices along the way. Upward Arcs should feature moments of relapse when a character surrenders to their weakness. Outward Arcs should reveal moments of doubt and frustration. Downward Arcs should include moments of hope before the eventual downfall.

While brainstorming your character's journey, list five possible good choices and five possible bad choices they might make. These highs and lows can create an emotional rhythm that keeps your audience invested until the final choice is made.

CHEAT SHEET

- Character Roles include Protagonist, Antagonist, Major Supporting Characters, Minor Characters, and Stock Characters.
- The four levels of deep and realistic characters are Goal, Motivation, Character Lie, and Tragic Backstory.
- To make characters engaging, create sympathy, empathy, or envy.
- Character arcs are internal journeys of transformation that explore how a character responds to their flaws and/or lies.
- A character flaw is a negative behavior or weakness that prevents a character from being happy.
- A character lie is a negative, misguided belief that a character holds about themselves, other people, or the world.
- In an Upward Arc a character believes a lie but grows to embrace a truth (they may also overcome a flaw).
- In an Outward Arc a character believes a truth and attempts to teach it to others.
- In a Downward Arc a character believes a truth but later embraces a lie (they may also succumb to a flaw).

CHAPTER 3
WORLDBUILDING

SOME OF YOU may be thinking: "Worldbuilding? I don't need to build a world. I don't write sci-fi or fantasy, so what's the point?"

The point is that *all* fiction requires worldbuilding. Sci-fi, fantasy, mysteries, thrillers, horror, romance, comedy, contemporary—every genre needs it. Even the 2010 movie *Buried*, which takes place inside a coffin, needs it. Though sci-fi and fantasy require the most extensive worldbuilding, every story relies on this key element.

It circles back to character. Whether we're crafting the next Middle Earth or a contemporary American office building, we must connect our world to our characters. Much like real-life human beings, fictional people should be impacted by where they grew up, where they currently live, and what goes on across the globe. To ignore worldbuilding is to ignore character.

In this chapter, we'll explore the four key components of worldbuilding, how this element enhances a narrative, and how to build a universe that comes to life through character.

THE FOUR COMPONENTS OF WORLDBUILDING

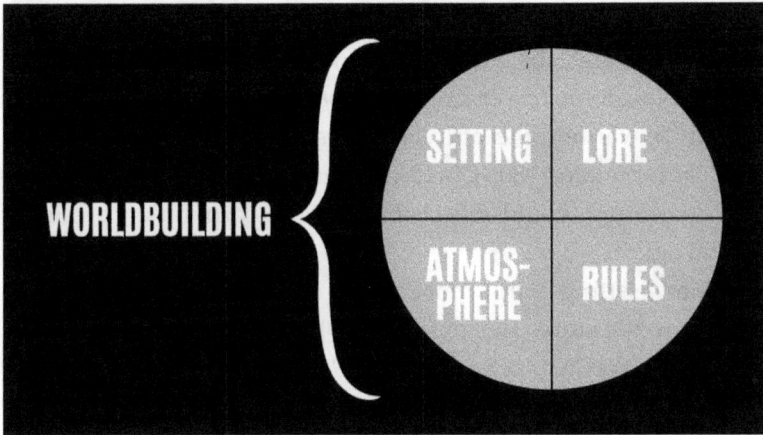

Many people mistakenly consider worldbuilding and setting as the same thing. While there is overlap, worldbuilding is more than just the setting. A fictional universe consists of four specific components.

SETTING

Setting refers to when and where a story takes place. Fictional universes are essentially limitless, but a story must occur at a specific point within that universe. For instance, the world of *Star Wars* contains numerous planets and billions of years of history, but *Star Wars: A New Hope* takes place mostly on Tatooine and the Death Star during year zero. The acclaimed video game *Star Wars: Knights of the Old Republic* is set four thousand years earlier, with events occurring across eleven different locations. Same universe, different setting.

Settings are essentially the story's present-day environment. This includes geography, landscapes, weather, plants, animals, cities, towns, and populations. Don't worry about history just yet; instead, consider what characters can immediately experience. If we were to step into Winterfell from *Game of Thrones*, we'd notice cold temperatures, warmly dressed townspeople, direwolves, and the Stark family banner. Alternatively, if we visited Nakatomi Tower from *Die Hard*, the Los Angeles weather would be warmer, the office workers would be dressed appropriately for a late-1980s Christmas party, and the building's interior decorating would reflect the tastes of corporation president Joe Takagi.

Good settings are more than backdrops—they're active players in the story. This means they both challenge and support characters. For instance, in *Jurassic Park* the island of Isla Nublar threatens the main cast with extreme weather, isolation, and live dinosaurs. The island also provides natural safe havens and park facilities where people can escape danger. Survival in *Jurassic Park* depends on how characters interact with this particular setting.

Lore

If setting is the present, lore is the past. Specifically, lore includes the histories, traditions, facts, and stories that are passed down within a fictional world. It might help to think of lore as the world's backstory.

Lore is a powerful tool because it makes a world seem larger than it appears on the page or screen. A basic setting might appear shallow on its own, but some carefully selected bits of lore can expand the world within the audience's mind. Think about when Harry Potter visits Ollivanders Wand Shop, which bears a sign reading "Makers of fine wands since 382 B.C." Or the moment in *Star Wars* when Obi-Wan first mentions Jedi Knights and the Clone Wars. Simple details like these expand the scope and possibilities of the world.

The purpose of lore is to deepen the universe and make it feel lived-in by people outside the main cast. We accomplish this by sharing small details that invite audiences to imagine the world's expansive history and past inhabitants. But be warned—we don't want to force-feed lore to the audience. Present-day characters should have a reason for reflecting on the past. If they do, lore becomes a natural part of the story-telling process.

Atmosphere

Setting is the present, lore is the past, and atmosphere is the emotional vibe generated by the two. Revealing a character's attitude toward the setting is a strong start for creating atmosphere, and lore contributes greater context and stakes. For example, the 1980 movie *The Shining* establishes its setting as a remote, isolated hotel filled with claustrophobic hallways and mysterious rooms. That's creepy stuff, and the atmosphere becomes outright terrifying when we factor in the lore about local burial grounds and how the hotel's previous caretaker went insane and murdered his family.

Atmosphere can range from severe to cozy. Intimate worlds like the Overlook Hotel from *The Shining* primarily stick to one particular mood. Larger worlds, by comparison, may offer more dynamic vibes. For instance, the *Lord of the Rings* films establish stunning landscapes while peppering in historical details that enrich the atmosphere of the whimsical Shire, the gloomy Mines of Moria, and the oppressive land of Mordor.

It's best to align the atmosphere with plot events, meaning that low-energy scenes will usually occur at lighthearted loca-tions while high-conflict events occur in more perilous locations. That said, atmosphere can always be tweaked with things like weather conditions and circumstances. A cozy campsite can become a danger zone if a storm brews and hungry animals growl nearby.

RULES AND SYSTEMS

Rules and systems organize the story world and provide a sense of logic, consistency, and order. Rules can be societal, cultural, political, scientific, or magical. What makes them interesting is how they empower and inhibit characters.

Many stories follow a "fish out of water" premise in which a character ventures into a new territory with unfamiliar rules. For instance, an American visiting Japan would have to account for societal and cultural differences, as well as laws about which items can be brought into the country. Likewise, someone visiting the moon would have to account for reduced gravity and the lack of breathable oxygen. When Harry Potter passes from the muggle world to the wizarding world, he must learn how to board Platform Nine-and-Three-Quarters, among other things.

Rules enhance a world's creativity by challenging characters to follow, circumvent, or outright break them in pursuit of goals. For example, the 2018 movie *A Quiet Place* is set in a post-apocalyptic world dominated by monsters that kill anyone who makes noise. This forces one family to live silently on a farm, and they must adapt when the mother is due to give birth. Compare that to the contemporary world of the 2014 movie *Whiplash*, in which a drummer enrolls at a prestigious music school where he must win the approval of a hostile instructor. In that environment, failure is punished with violent outbursts, emotional abuse, and the loss of a lifelong dream.

ACTION STEPS: BUILDING A WORLD

STEP #1: Pick a starting point

Ask yourself, "What kind of world am I creating and why?" A story's genre and concept will usually dictate what type of universe is required. For example, an epic fantasy story might include breathtaking locations and a robust magic system; a haunted house tale might limit itself to one location and focus on the lore that caused the haunting.

Often, the easiest way to begin the worldbuilding process is to embrace one of the four components—whichever calls out to you. Maybe it's a specific location or historical nugget, an atmospheric vibe, or the rules of a futuristic society. Whatever appeals, start writing about it. Exploring one component will help develop the others.

STEP #2: Decide how your world and characters shape each other

Worldbuilding should influence characters. Ask yourself how the setting, lore, atmosphere, and rules affect your main cast. Keep in mind that the world should offer both challenges and support. Woodland terrain, for instance, might cause your character to become lost while also serving as a hiding place from enemies.

Additionally, characters should reshape the world—particularly the setting and the rules. In relation to setting, it might mean burning down a neighbor's house or revitalizing a city slum. Regarding rules, your character might undermine an existing system or take control of a power structure.

STEP #3: Give your world a test-run

Some writers prefer to craft their world before writing the actual story. There's nothing wrong with this approach, but one mistake these writers tend to make is obsessing over every last worldbuilding detail before starting the story. This is referred to as "worldbuilding disease" and it leaves many writers bedridden—or at least prevents them from writing that novel they've always dreamed of.

The cure is to write **test scenes** every now and then. Simply drop a character into your universe, give them a basic goal, then let them interact with the world. While writing these scenes, you may notice certain parts of your world are dull, inconsistent, or incomplete. That's okay. Recognizing these weaknesses now will provide direction as you fine-tune your universe.

WORLDBUILDING: THE FORGOTTEN CHARACTER

The secret to writing a better world is treating it like a legitimate character, a member of the supporting cast. This means asking "How does it impact characters?" and "How is it impacted by them?" Characters may view the world as an ally or opponent, as inspiring or imposing, as something to be protected or controlled. Exploring this relationship generates plot possibilities —and if you're ever lacking conflict, look to involve the setting.

At minimum, characters should color the world with emotion. In other words, personal attitudes should shape and enrich the world. If a protagonist returns home for Christmas, they should view their hometown subjectively. Do they see a safe haven or danger zone? Are the Christmas lights appropriately festive or annoyingly bright? Are the local restaurants filled with mouth-watering aromas or nauseating stenches? In the realm of worldbuilding, characters' subjective interpretations are just as important as factual details.

Think about *Batman Begins*. The movie involves Batman and Ra's al Ghul battling for control of Gotham City. Batman views Gotham as his responsibility, the home and legacy he's obligated to protect. Ra's, meanwhile, views Gotham as a cancer—a diseased hellscape that must be cured through destruction. These opposing attitudes fuel the central conflict while creating a more complex city. When Batman defeats his enemy at the movie's climax, Batman's perception of Gotham becomes the new reality.

CONNECTING WORLDBUILDING TO CHARACTER DEVELOPMENT

Worldbuilding serves as an extension of a character's status or emotional state. Basic examples of this might involve an unfulfilled billionaire living in an empty mansion or a grieving wife visiting a rainy cemetery. As emotional states change, the world should adapt to signal the shift in mood. That means our lonely billionaire may search for companionship at a lively festival, while the grieving wife notices the sun coming out when a friend joins her in mourning.

Worldbuilding can also reflect a character's development. In *The Anatomy of Story*, John Truby notes that "in the vast majority of stories, the hero's overall change moves from slavery to freedom. If that's true in your story, the visual world will probably move from slavery to freedom as well." This is common in Upward Arcs, in which the protagonist is introduced at an undesirable location. For example:

- In *Harry Potter and the Sorcerer's Stone*, Harry wakes up in a cramped closet beneath the staircase.
- In *Star Wars*, Luke Skywalker is introduced on his uncle's desert farm.
- In *The Terminator*, Sarah Conner is stuck working a dead-end job at a diner.

As these characters grow, their environments change with them. Small amounts of freedom are gained, but the antagonists hold power:

- In *Harry Potter and the Sorcerer's Stone*, Harry attends Hogwarts and encounters new friends, hostile enemies, and shifty professors who test his abilities.
- In *Star Wars*, Luke leaves the farm but enters a world dominated by the Empire.
- In *The Terminator*, Sarah is chased by a murderous robot sent from a future world. To survive, she must flee to various safe havens in Los Angeles.

Finally, the characters complete their arcs and are rewarded with better worlds:

- In *Harry Potter and the Sorcerer's Stone*, Harry defeats Voldemort and wins the love of his Hogwarts classmates.
- In *Star Wars*, Luke destroys the Death Star and finds his place among the Rebels.
- In *The Terminator*, Sarah destroys the Terminator, then later drives off with her unborn son to prepare for the future war.

When crafting character arcs, consider how the story world changes alongside the protagonist. Not only can this signal a shift in the protagonist's emotional state, but it can also emphasize how the character is impacting the world (or vice versa).

ACTION STEPS: MERGING WORLD WITH CHARACTER

STEP #1: Include the world on your character web

In the previous chapter we talked about building a character web that includes your main cast. Now you'll want to include your world as a bonus character. Add it to the web, then draw connections. Figure out how each character uniquely responds to it.

For more detailed results, include each worldbuilding component on the web. Setting, lore, atmosphere, and rules should affect characters in different ways. Maybe a side character enjoys the energetic atmosphere but hates the humid weather. Maybe your antagonist respects the world's lore but hates the present-day rules.

STEP #2: Decide how your world reflects your character's internal journey

Ideally, the setting should reflect your character's mood and status. Darker settings, for instance, may represent a character's gloomy or fearful mindset, while idyllic settings may signal their hope. But don't let settings be static—remember, the sun can rise on a dark location, and enemies can terrorize a pleasant one.

Going beyond setting, consider using lore to create an atmospheric vibe that signals your character's internal struggle. For example, a rookie cop intent on taking down the mob might second guess himself after learning what the mob did to the last officer who tried to play hero.

Finally, consider rules and systems. A dorky girl may want to fit in with the cool kids at school, but that will require her to contend with the social hierarchy and the expectations that accompany it. The rules may overpower her early on, but as she learns the game, she can rewrite the rules herself.

BRINGING THE STORY WORLD TO LIFE

Not every fictional universe needs to be as meticulously designed as Middle Earth or Westeros. Sometimes it's enough to drop us into modern-day Cleveland and let things rip. Whether we're working with the visionary or the mundane, we bring that world to life on the page or screen by carefully selecting details that invite the audience in.

Some writers make the mistake of introducing their universe by unloading every world-related detail they can think of. Bad idea. Not only does this overwhelm even the most patient audiences, but it also snuffs out the sense of discovery. Audiences don't want everything mapped out for them—they want to experience worldbuilding the way they might experience an uncharted island or a secret entrance behind a bookcase. In other words, they want to participate.

Rather than carelessly unloading details, we should express relevant aspects while characters naturally interact with the environment. This can be accomplished by using sensory details, limiting expository info, and hinting at a larger universe.

Sensory Details

Transporting an audience to another world is only possible by way of the five senses. Sight, sound, feeling, smell, and taste are the magic spells that connect audiences to imaginary locations. Not only do we need to introduce settings through the five senses—to maintain a fictional reality, we must keep providing fresh details.

Whenever characters enter a new area, it's our job to describe what that character experiences. For instance, say a Los Angeles detective enters an apartment where a murder has been committed, and he notices sights like the decomposing body, the murder weapon, and signs of struggle. That's a good start, but we need more. Next our detective notices sounds: street traffic, yelling neighbors, etc. Then he feels warm, humid air and sweat trailing down his back. He smells rotting flesh and spoiled Chinese food in the kitchen. Finally, he tastes the cigarette he stubbed out ten minutes ago.

If we're writing for the screen, our script will primarily focus on sights and sounds, but we can also show what a character feels, smells, and tastes. If our detective lifts a couch to check for evidence, he might grimace and reach for his back—a sure sign of bodily pain. If he pinches his nose, that indicates a horrible stench. If he later drinks coffee and winces at the first sip, we know it's not gourmet brew.

We can also use dialogue to express a character's sensory experience. A simple comment about the apartment smelling like rotten strawberries can enliven the world. Just make sure not to overuse this dialogue technique—if characters talk incessantly about smells and tastes, it'll feel forced.

Limiting Expository Info

Though worldbuilding can sprawl in endless directions, explaining every detail will only weigh the story down. For that reason, we limit what we tell the audience. This means having characters interact with relevant info that the audience needs to know at a given time.

If we're writing about an NYPD detective who's trying to locate a kidnapped child, we don't provide a tour of every street in New York City. Instead, we might focus on locations where the child was last seen. When the detective visits them, she'll notice aspects of the setting that are relevant to the kidnapping—nearby playgrounds, schools, etc. She'll reflect on the history of the area—especially changing crime patterns. Finally, she'll think about the rules and systems that organize these locations. Do crime bosses control these streets? Would gang members have a motive for kidnapping a child? Would someone else—someone more powerful?

Another challenge to be wary of is **info dumps**, or lengthy explanations of backstory. Though it's tempting to unload worldbuilding in large chunks, it's typically better to weave such info into dramatic scenes. For example, when *Game of Thrones* opens, we don't get a lengthy description of Westeros. Instead, we meet a group of men charged with protecting the Wall. They encounter a mysterious White Walker, and two men are murdered before the survivor runs to warn others. This prologue brings the world to life through drama—which is preferable to a lengthy info dump. More importantly, we experience the world from a character's perspective. The personal stakes of life and death engage us and spur our curiosity as we learn about a small section of Westeros and the lethal creatures inhabiting it.

Now, info dumps aren't always evil. Sometimes we need to unload **exposition**—or key background details—in a short period of time. We can keep an info dump from falling flat by making the audience *want* the info before we deliver it.

The Terminator does this by first getting us invested in its characters. We wonder "Why is this killing machine chasing Sarah Connor, of all people? What's so special about her?" Later, when Sarah and her protector Kyle Reese are hiding in a parking garage, Reese reveals critical worldbuilding info about the Terminator and the future war. By this point, both Sarah and the audience want these details, and the info dump proves engaging rather than boring.

Hinting at a Larger Universe

Though we want to limit the worldbuilding details we provide, we don't want to make our world feel small. That's why it's important to select details that suggest a larger world exists beyond the page or screen. This enables the audience to actively participate in the worldbuilding process by imagining components that may or may not appear within the story.

Imagine a small town. On the surface it's a few dozen houses encircled by trees. But if we introduce characters who mention growing up elsewhere or how they hope to move to a nearby city someday, suddenly this small town becomes part of a larger world.

Consider the 2014 revenge-thriller *John Wick*. When John, a former assassin, comes out of retirement and reenters the criminal underworld, he uses special coins to pay for services like disposing of dead bodies. Though it's never explained how he earned coins or how this underground economy functions, audiences are welcome to fill in these details themselves. When John visits the Continental Hotel, he encounters numerous other assassins. Only a few impact the movie's plot, but the abundance of killers suggests that murders are being carried out across the globe. Such details create a lively world without bloating the movie's runtime or disrupting its pacing.

ACTION STEPS: INJECTING LIFE INTO YOUR WORLD

STEP #1: Engage the five senses

Most writers have no trouble incorporating sight, but the other four senses can be tricky. You may have to rethink a character's perspective to activate the other four, but most settings offer adequate sensory input.

If your setting doesn't offer sounds, sensations, smells, and tastes, you can always import those details from outside events and characters. For example, a static living room can come alive if stormy weather rattles the windows and sends the family dog hopping onto your protagonist's lap. The dog's body heat and the odor of unwashed fur invite more sensory interaction. From there, find a taste. Is the protagonist eating something? Chewing gum? Tasting salt on the coastal air? Coughing up blood? There are many possibilities.

STEP #2: Lead with drama while limiting expository info

An excellent way to introduce a world is to reveal it through characters. Allow them to live their lives and chase their goals. Then look for opportunities to weave in worldbuilding. Have your character notice sensory details, overhear bits of lore, react to the atmosphere, or encounter people who impose the world's rules.

One tried-but-true technique is to drop a character into an unfamiliar location and have them discover the world along with the audience. As the story alternates between plot events and worldbuilding details, it makes the learning process feel natural and creates a bond between the point-of-view character and the audience.

STEP #3: Condense info dumps into "hardworking" details

There's no shame in writing an info dump, but when you reread your work, decide if you can shrink a massive explanation down to a single detail. Try mentioning parts of the world rather than the whole. Then leave room for curiosity so the audience can explore the world as much as they desire.

For example, instead of rambling on about all the dangerous

monsters that inhabit the forest north of town, have a reckless teenager venture out there and disappear. Or, instead of overexplaining the history of your fantasy world's royal lineage, have the local blacksmith gloat about how he personally forged the sword that cut off the previous ruler's head.

CHEAT SHEET

- Worldbuilding is a necessity in all fiction, not just sci-fi and fantasy.
- Worldbuilding includes the following four components:
  - Setting: the present-day environment.
  - Lore: the histories, traditions, and facts passed down within the world.
  - Atmosphere: the emotional vibe created by setting, lore, and characters' attitudes.
  - Rules and Systems: the societal, cultural, scientific, or magical rules that organize the world and give it a sense of logic and consistency.
- Worldbuilding acts like a major character that influences—and is influenced by—other characters.
- Worldbuilding details often reflect a character's emotional state. As characters continue along their personal journeys, the world is revealed in wider scope.
- Story worlds are brought to life through:
  - Using the five senses.
  - Limiting exposition to relevant details.
  - Providing hints that encourage audiences to imagine a larger universe beyond the page or screen.

CHAPTER 4
THEME

THEME IS the soul of a story, the meaning beneath the surface. It's the lesson, the message, the truth. Though character and plot determine *what* happens in a narrative, theme determines *why* imaginary people and events matter to the audience.

In his book *Story Engineering*, Larry Brooks argues that "Theme is the *relevance* of your story to life." In other words, theme is the bridge that connects fiction and reality. Fictionalized experiences matter because they reflect similar experiences in human realities. Stories guide us through imaginary worlds filled with truth, and that truth is what makes the journey worthwhile.

This chapter will focus on understanding and creating strong themes. We'll explore what theme is, how it enriches a narrative, and how to effectively generate meaning within our fiction.

THE PURPOSE OF THEME

Theme is an abstract storytelling element, which means we can't see theme the same way we see a character like Batman or a plot event like the Joker blowing up a hospital. Rather, theme hides within the story and emerges through action, dialogue, and situation.

What *is* the definition of theme? Well, that's where things get messy. Some definitions claim that theme is a basic idea, like love, redemption, or adolescence. Others paint theme as a central argument like "security vs. freedom" or "knowledge vs. wisdom." Theme might also be defined as an underlying message, such as "Revenge leads to destruction" or "It's never too late to chase your dreams."

All these definitions are valid, and that's why theme can be a tricky element to grasp. Should we think of it as a broad idea or a specific truth? Is it a message characters express or an argument characters take sides on? Though multiple definitions offer flexibility, they can also leave us feeling confused, scatterbrained, and hesitant to write.

But relax—rather than stressing out over definitions, we're going to focus on a more practical approach to theme. Specifically, we'll examine its three key purposes.

THEMATIC PURPOSE #1: THEME AS A QUESTION THAT DEMANDS ANSWERS

If you survived high school, you might've been taught that theme is the moral or message of a story. School teachers often push this particular definition because it allows a book's theme to be scribbled down as an answer on a test sheet—something like "Ambition leads to destruction" or "The powerful must protect the innocent."

Thinking of theme as a summation isn't necessarily a bad thing, but we writers are better off thinking of theme as a question.

Why? Because **questions energize the brainstorming process**. They act as a launching pad for character, worldbuilding, and plot, and they shape the story's trajectory. In other words, when we designate a theme as the central question, the story becomes a series of answers.

This is why we don't want to build theme around a flat statement like "Ambition leads to destruction." Such statements flatten creativity. Instead, try rephrasing the theme as a question —something like "Can ambition lead to destruction?" or "What is the cost of ambition?" or "Where does unchecked ambition lead?" These questions demand answers. They generate creative sparks that crackle.

Here are some popular stories and their central thematic questions:

- *Jurassic Park*: "Should man tamper with nature?"
- *Star Wars: A New Hope*: "Is hope enough to defeat a superior enemy?"
- *The Dark Knight*: "How far must lawful people go to impose order on a chaotic world?"
- *Rocky*: "Is it ever too late to become a winner?"
- *Good Will Hunting*: "What makes life worth living— success, happiness, or safety?"

Notice how these questions generate possibilities? They promise conflict, dilemmas, and character interaction—all of which engage audiences.

In practice, a story's thematic question is typically raised early on, whether through action, dialogue, or situation. From there, the story delivers answers. A narrative should offer at least two answers, and they should repeatedly come into conflict like lawyers in a courtroom. Both sides present evidence and argue their points until we reach a definitive answer at the end.

Jurassic Park tackles the question "Should man tamper with nature?" by exploring two answers: yes and no. On one hand, tampering with nature can lead to positive things like resurrecting extinct species, bolstering economic growth, and providing educational opportunities. On the other hand, tampering with nature can also lead to greed, turmoil, and destruction.

In the movie, park owner John Hammond represents the "Yes" answer; scientists Alan Grant, Ellie Sattler, and Ian Malcom represent the "No." Early on, characters debate this question during lunch, and afterward the story explores the question in deeper detail. *Jurassic Park* embodies both sides of the argument, presenting the wonders of live dinosaurs while also revealing the damage that ancient reptiles (and their modern creators) can cause. In the end, the story leans toward the final answer of "No."

THEMATIC PURPOSE #2: THEME AS A UNIFYING IDEA

In addition to creating meaning, theme also creates cohesiveness. It serves as the unseen glue that holds the other story elements together. If we think of our central theme as a question, then the story becomes a series of relevant answers. Keyword: relevant. Theme determines which characters belong in the story, where it takes place, how the plot progresses, and everything in between.

Let's return to *Jurassic Park* and its thematic question: "Should man tamper with nature?" In order to build an engaging story from this question, we must connect it to relevant characters. First, we need someone willing to tamper with nature, and that's where John Hammond comes in. He's the ultra-rich businessman who sets the plot in motion by cloning dinosaurs.

Next, we need protagonists who oppose him. Enter the scientists Alan Grant, Ellie Sattler, and Ian Malcom. Offering scientific expertise, they express concern over the consequences of cloning.

Finally, we need supporting characters, like Hammond's grandkids and his key staff members, who contribute their own answers to the thematic question. At first, Hammond's grand-kids love the idea of a dinosaur theme park, but their attitude changes when they face mortal danger. Likewise, the staff members initially welcome the opportunity to work at Jurassic Park, but later they are eaten alive by Hammond's creations.

In addition to shaping characters, theme also brings focus to the central plot. *Jurassic Park* is a horror story at its core, and in many horror stories, characters who commit a particular "sin" are punished. In this case, those who tamper with nature are punished with death. Five people die in *Jurassic Park*, and each stands on the wrong side of the story's theme. The victims include:

- Jophery Brown, the park worker who is eaten by a raptor in the opening scene
- Donald Gennaro, the profit-hungry lawyer who is devoured by a T-Rex
- Dennis Nedry, the computer programmer who steals dinosaur embryos and is later eaten by a Dilophosaurus
- John Arnold, the system engineer who's killed off-screen by a raptor
- Robert Muldoon, the game warden who's killed by an especially clever raptor

In addition to these five victims, John Hammond suffers a metaphorical death when his entrepreneurial dreams are crushed. The park itself dies, though Hammond himself survives because he admits his mistakes and vows to shut down the park.

THEMATIC PURPOSE #3: THEME AS A LESSON

In Chapter 2, we discussed character arcs, the internal journeys that characters undergo while wrestling with personal flaws and lies. Overcoming a flaw or lie requires a character to learn a lesson, which can explore the story's theme.

The movie *Rocky* poses the question "Is it ever too late to become a winner?" Club boxer Rocky Balboa initially believes he isn't worthy of respect. He fights like a bum, lives like a bum, and works like a bum while collecting money for the mob. Over the course of the movie, however, he gains self-respect by pursuing a romantic relationship with Adrian and rising to the challenge against heavyweight champ Apollo Creed. Though Rocky doesn't defeat Creed, he achieves his goal of becoming the first man to last fifteen rounds against the champ. Thus, Rocky gains self-respect and becomes a winner by rejuvenating his life.

We've analyzed *Jurassic Park*'s themes extensively, but let's take one more gander. This time, we'll examine three characters and how their arcs connect with the central theme. Note that all three lessons explore the question "Should man tamper with nature?" And each character is rewarded or punished based on how they grapple with their lesson.

Alan Grant learns a lesson about valuing children. Initially he believes kids are a nuisance, but after interacting with Hammond's grandchildren, he learns to cherish them. This is significant because human nature requires that the old protect the young, and Alan opts to not tamper with this aspect of nature. Ultimately, he and the children help each other survive.

Dennis Nedry, meanwhile, fails to learn a lesson about resisting greed. He intends to betray his employer by stealing dinosaur embryos and delivering them to a competitor, which would make cloning more commonplace. Ultimately, however, Nedry fails to escape with the embryos. After compromising the park's security system and endangering everyone on the island, he meets a deadly fate.

Finally, John Hammond learns a hard lesson in hubris. The movie opens with him believing himself to be the creator of the next Disney Land, but his reckless ambition gives rise to a night-mare. After recognizing the consequences of tampering with nature, he renounces his choices and meets a bittersweet end in which his dream dies but he and his grandkids survive.

ACTION STEPS: BUILDING A PURPOSEFUL THEME

STEP #1: Choose a theme

There's no magic formula for identifying the perfect theme. The best you can do is live life and pay attention to what inspires, engages, or bothers you, reflecting on the paths you travel, the mistakes you make, the lessons you learn. Life offers many potential themes, and you must decide which truth best fits your story.

Writers take various approaches to incorporating theme into their work. Some select a theme up front and merge it with a story concept. Others discover the theme during the writing process, sometimes even after completing a first draft.

If you're struggling to conjure a theme, examine some of your favorite stories. Determine what themes they explore and try borrowing or reinventing those thematic ideas. Once you find a theme that excites you, roll with it.

STEP #2: Frame your theme as a question

Theme can emerge from the simplest ideas, like love, hope, illness, adolescence, or revenge. Whatever idea calls to you, frame it as a question. Instead of working with the theme of "parenthood," consider raising questions like "What sacrifices must parents make while raising children?" or "How far will parents go to give their children a better life?"

When crafting a thematic question, consider how the question can shape the narrative. For example, let's say we're writing a revenge story. Our thematic question might be "How does revenge lead to destruction?" This question shapes the story by promising destruction. It suggests a tragic ending and much suffering along the way. Alternatively, we might rewrite the question as "How does revenge lead to healing?" This revised question promises a happier ending, with moments of relief leading to the finale.

STEP #3: Connect other story elements and ideas to your theme

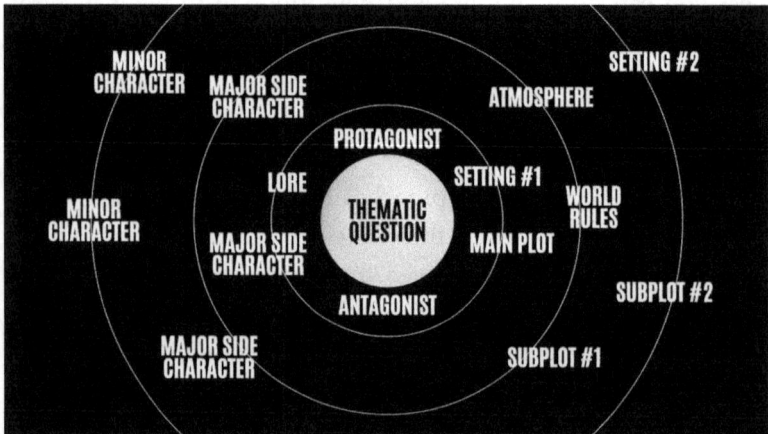

Once you've identified a thematic question to build around, think of it as the center of the story's universe. It may help to picture a solar system where the thematic question acts as the sun that pulls in specific characters, worldbuilding details, and plot events. The more relevant the idea, the closer it'll be to the center of the map. For example, a protagonist who consistently seeks to answer the thematic question would be close to the center, while a comedic subplot that barely explores the theme might nudge the outer ring. Those closest to the center are worth developing; those farther away should be revised or cut.

STEP #4: Determine how your theme rewards and punishes characters

When crafting character arcs, think of theme as a judge that rewards or punishes characters based on their choices. Those who follow the story's **thematic "code"** are rewarded while those who violate it are punished.

Say our thematic question is "How does revenge lead to destruction?" In this case, the "code" states that those who pursue revenge must be destroyed. So if two characters pursue revenge, both should face punishment in unique ways. Alternatively, if one character pursues revenge and the second opposes revenge, the first character should suffer while the second is rewarded. And if we add a third character who's initially tempted by revenge but ultimately rejects it, that character should face punishment before being rewarded at the end.

CONNECTING CHARACTER AND THEME

Many writers stress out over choosing the right characters for a particular story, especially when determining whether a supporting character truly belongs. If you're struggling with this dilemma, here's some good news: theme can narrow down the selection process.

Once you've created a cast of characters, ask whether they each connect with the central theme. Do they help answer the thematic question? Do they gel with the unifying idea? Does their arc teach a relevant lesson? If so, they belong.

Remember that each character should contribute to the theme in a unique way. We don't want every character undergoing the same thematic journey—that would be redundant and diminish the theme's impact. Instead, we want characters who engage the theme from different angles.

When connecting characters to theme, start with the protagonist and antagonist. They'll line up on opposite sides of the thematic question. If the protagonist represents a "Yes" answer, the antagonist champions "No." Then each character takes action, creating a back-and-forth battle that explores the question.

But a one-on-one battle won't hold our interest for long. We need to mix in supporting characters to add variety and nuance, while also impacting how the protagonist and antagonist approach the theme.

For example, consider *The Dark Knight*'s thematic question "How far must lawful people go to impose order on a chaotic world?" In this movie Batman fights crime while adhering to strict moral principles. He protects the innocent, refuses to kill, and uses fear to neutralize criminals. His answer is "Lawful people must preserve their morals while imposing order."

Then along comes the Joker, who believes such principles are a joke. He terrorizes the innocent, kills without hesitation, and creates his own twisted culture of fear and violence. His answer is "Lawful people must abandon their morals to impose order."

As the conflict escalates, the Joker tests Batman by creating dilemmas that deepen our understanding of the theme. When the Joker threatens to kill hostages until Batman reveals his secret identity, Batman faces a brutal dilemma. If he resists, innocent people will die; if he surrenders, he'll be thrown in jail, unable to stop the Joker. This dilemma compels Batman to seek counsel from his butler Alfred (a major supporting character), who urges Batman to resist.

Shortly afterward, district attorney Harvey Dent takes the fall for Batman. Harvey is the movie's chief supporting character, and he contributes a nuanced answer to the thematic question. Whereas Batman believes in upholding morals and the Joker believes in abandoning them, Harvey proves flexible. Though he initially believes in the rule of law, personal trauma shatters his belief. Before long, he's flipping coins to decide whether criminals should live or die. His answer is "Lawful people must occasionally use unlawful means to impose order." Later, while attempting to pass judgment, Harvey is killed, which signals that he deviated too far from the story's thematic code.

THEMATIC QUESTION:
"How far must lawful people go to impose order on a chaotic world?"

BATMAN:	THE JOKER:
"PRESERVE MORALS"	"ABANDON MORALS"

HARVEY DENT:
"FLEXIBLE MORALS"

ACTION STEPS: CONNECTING THEME TO CHARACTER

STEP #1: Draw connections between theme and characters

There are two basic approaches here. The first is to create characters and allow theme to naturally emerge during the drafting process. Once a theme emerges, recognize it and find ways to strengthen the thematic bond. You can achieve this by paying attention to similarities in characters' journeys. If multiple characters are seeking revenge, zero in on the theme of revenge and explore the different sacrifices characters make while attempting to achieve it.

Another approach is to choose a specific theme from the get-go and build characters from the theme. This enables you to assemble your main cast with the theme in mind, which can potentially save time and headaches.

STEP # 2: Revise or cut characters who don't jive with the theme

After completing your first draft, identify your characters and determine which fit the theme. For example, if you're writing a story about revenge, make sure the major characters have a connection to revenge—whether they want it, oppose it, regret it, etc. If a major character doesn't explore the theme, either revise or cut the character.

STEP # 3: Have characters express the theme in a natural way

One of the biggest mistakes writers make is expressing the theme through on-the-nose dialogue. If characters run around saying, "Revenge is bad!" the theme will come off as ham-fisted and laughable.

Instead, seek compelling ways to implement the theme. Have the protagonist wrestle with internal conflict. Have them debate their plans with a close friend. Have them attempt to go through with a vengeful act while facing and overcoming obstacles. Then have them make a final choice to answer the thematic question— which brings us to our next topic...

CLIMACTIC CHOICES: THE FINAL ANSWER TO THE THEMATIC QUESTION

We've discussed how a strong thematic question compels characters to provide answers. Good stories explore answers through conflict, but eventually the conflict must end. That's when the protagonist makes a **climactic choice**—one that should work on multiple storytelling levels. The choice should not only decide the outcome of the plot and the protagonist's arc, it should also deliver the final answer to the thematic question.

Identifying your story's final answer should be relatively simple. In many cases, "Yes" or "No" will suffice. For instance, *Star Wars: A New Hope* poses the question, "Is hope enough to defeat a superior enemy?" In the film's climactic dogfight sequence, Luke answers "Yes" by using the Force to blow up the Death Star. Hope destroys the Empire's weapon and saves the Rebel Alliance from annihilation.

In some cases, instead of "Yes" or "No," the protagonist may have three or more options. *Good Will Hunting*'s question is "What makes life worth living—success, happiness, or safety?" At the climax Will chooses between three options: the certainty of a lucrative career in mathematics, the risky pursuit of romantic love, and the comfortable status quo of living among Boston's working class. These three options tempt and torment him until he chooses to pursue happiness with his girlfriend Skylar.

But what if your question is more open-ended than the previous examples? *The Dark Knight* explores the question "How far must lawful people go to impose order on a chaotic world?" A basic "Yes" or "No" answer won't work here. That said, the movie nonetheless provides a straightforward answer.

In the climax Batman encounters a corrupted Harvey Dent, who has been committing murders across Gotham. Their final confrontation leads to Harvey's death, as well as a bigger problem: not only is Harvey's once-immaculate reputation in ruins, but his actions could undo the progress he made against organized crime while serving as the city's prosecutor.

To avoid letting droves of criminals off the hook, Batman decides to take the blame for Harvey's murders, thus preserving the man's reputation and neutralizing organized crime. The movie's final answer then becomes "Lawful people must make sacrifices to impose order on a chaotic world."

ACTION STEPS: PROVIDING THE FINAL ANSWER

STEP #1: Determine the appropriate Climactic Answer

Depending on how open-ended your thematic question is, its answer might boil down to a simple yes or no, or it might include several possibilities.

In most stories, the protagonist makes the "right" choice, which delivers a happy ending. There are, of course, tragic outcomes as well, and if your protagonist makes the "wrong" choice, you need to punish them. Other major characters should also be rewarded or punished, depending on whether they adhere to the story's thematic code.

Ultimately, it's the writer who determines the code, and not every story needs to play out predictably. Though many stories reward honest characters while punishing liars, you can do the opposite and create a world where honesty leads to suffering and deception leads to glory. As long as you're consistent, either way can work.

STEP #2: Bridge the gap between the thematic question and climactic answer

Many writers struggle to navigate the middle of their story. One way to overcome this is by nailing down your thematic question and climactic answer. Doing so allows the middle to come into focus.

Let's say our question is "Does revenge create happiness?" and the final answer is "No." In this case, the story's middle should explore the conflict between "Yes" and "No." "Yes" moments might show revenge bringing temporary relief, but that will be followed by "No" moments where revenge leads to deeper suffering. From there, the thematic struggle continues, punch after counterpunch, until the final answer arrives with a decisive "No" that harshly punishes the protagonist.

We'll discuss more strategies for mapping out stories in Chapter 6 when we examine structure. For now, list five or more potential events that showcase your story's back-and-forth thematic struggle.

CHEAT SHEET

- Theme is an abstract, unseen story element that creates meaning. It bridges the gap between fiction and reality by expressing relevant real-life ideas, lessons, and truths.
- Thematic Question: The underlying question at the heart of a story. Characters provide answers to this question through their actions, choices, and personal journeys.
- Unifying Idea: Theme determines which characters, plot lines, settings, etc. are relevant to the story.
- Character Arc Lesson: When characters overcome (or succumb to) their flaws and / or lies, they learn valuable lessons that teach audiences how to live.
- Thematic Code: Unspoken rule that determines which characters are rewarded or punished in a particular story.
- Climatic Choice: A character's final choice that determines the outcome of the story and provides a decisive answer to the thematic question.

CHAPTER 5
PLOT

BELIEVE IT OR NOT, plot and story aren't the same thing. Audiences often mistake the two as interchangeable, but plot is a critical aspect of the overall story.

On the most basic level, plot is a **sequence of events that follows a pattern of cause and effect**—meaning that when characters take action, other characters react. This pattern creates conflict, which forces the opposing sides to battle back and forth until the conflict is resolved.

On a deeper level, plot serves as an external representation of a character's internal journey. This means that if our protagonist grows from being cowardly to brave, the plot must represent that journey with appropriate events, such as the protagonist confronting a bully, climbing a dangerous mountain, or banishing ghosts from a haunted house.

In this chapter we'll discuss plot, how it functions, and how to engage an audience with external events. We won't tackle plot structure just yet, but don't worry—that's coming up in Chapter 6.

THREE TYPES OF PLOTS: OVERARCHING, CENTRAL, AND SUBPLOTS

Every story needs at least one plot; in most cases, one won't be enough. That's because audiences can easily burn out on a single sequence of events. For instance, imagine if *The Terminator* was nothing but Sarah Connor running and hiding from danger. The movie would certainly start off exciting, but before long the novelty would fade, and we would grow sick of the cat-and-mouse routine.

Thankfully, *The Terminator* doesn't rely on a single plot line. Instead it includes others that explore the Future War, Sarah's personal life, and the LAPD's efforts to stop the Terminator. These ancillary plots not only keep the movie fresh, they also add complexity, unpredictability, and meaning. They transform a simple chase into an epic battle for the fate of humanity.

To create and manage plot lines, we need to understand the three main types of plots: overarching, central, and subplots. Each bears different responsibilities, so let's break them down.

OVERARCHING PLOTS

If we're writing a trilogy or series, we might include a long-term plot that stretches from the series' beginning to its conclusion. Typically, an overarching plot is something grand and difficult to resolve, like the war for the Iron Throne in *Game of Thrones*, the galactic war in *Star Wars*, or Batman's ongoing struggle against crime in Gotham.

Overarching plots create purpose and cohesiveness. They also provide a steady source of conflict, even when they're not the main focus of the story. In fact, it's common for an overarching plot to shift into the background while smaller, more immediate plots absorb the spotlight. As smaller plots are resolved, the overarching plot keeps the story humming along by maintaining conflict, stakes, and meaning.

CENTRAL PLOTS

Every story requires a central plot, which contains the main conflict and other key events. Unlike overarching plots, which may last for the duration of a series, central plots are more immediate and self-contained. They are usually resolved at the end of a given story, although in some cases they may be extended thanks to a "To be continued" scenario. If you're having trouble distinguishing between overarching and central plots, think of the overarching as a war and the central as a battle within the war.

Most central plots involve the protagonist trying to defeat the antagonist. In *Star Wars: A New Hope,* Luke destroys the Empire's Death Star. In *John Wick,* John gets revenge on the Russian mob. In *Alien,* Ellen Ripley defeats the deadly Xenomorph. Some stories may not have a true antagonist, in which case the central plot may involve two protagonists opposing each other. For example, the rom com *When Harry Met Sally* has no antagonist; instead, the titular characters bump into each other repeatedly until they become friends and eventually lovers.

You may be wondering, "Can a story have more than one central plot?"

It sure can. This is common in large-scale stories with multiple main characters. The first season of *Game of Thrones* has three central plots. One involves Ned Stark trying to expose the Lannisters as illegitimate rulers. Another involves Jon Snow finding his place in the Night's Watch. The third involves Daenerys Targaryen learning to become queen of the Dothraki. Though you can argue that Ned's plot takes top priority, each functions as a central plot and contributes to the overarching war for the Iron Throne.

SUBPLOTS

The central plot alone usually won't keep an audience hooked. For that reason, it helps to introduce at least one subplot—or supporting plot—to create variety and complexity. Subplots play a critical role in developing characters, managing the narrative's pacing, and providing comic relief, among other things.

Newer writers often struggle to identify subplots within a story, but here's an easy trick. First, identify the central plot, or main conflict between the protagonist and antagonist. From there, look for smaller conflicts that involve supporting characters. These secondary conflicts involve a relationship—romantic or otherwise—that challenges characters to grow. Popular subplots involve mentors, romantic partners, friends, family, and coworkers.

One or more characters may change because of a subplot. For example, *Star Wars: A New Hope* contains both a mentor subplot and friendship subplot. In the mentor subplot, Obi-Wan teaches Luke the ways of the Force, which enables Luke to trust his abilities and destroy the Death Star. In the friendship subplot, Luke challenges Han Solo to shed his selfish attitude, which prompts Han to help Luke during the Death Star battle. Both subplots not only contribute to character growth, but they significantly impact the central plot and determine the story's outcome.

ACTION STEPS: SELECTING YOUR PLOTS

STEP #1: Determine your central plot

Every story needs a central plot, which requires a compelling main conflict. The easiest way to craft one is by pitting your protagonist against an antagonist. Give the protagonist a story goal, then have their opponent create obstacles that prevent the protagonist from achieving that goal. If your story doesn't have an antagonist, look for other sources of conflict like nature, technology, health issues, internal conflict, etc.

STEP #2: Include subplots

Unless you're writing flash fiction, you'll want to include subplots that develop relationships between the protagonist and supporting characters. To get the most out of a subplot, ensure that it impacts characters' journeys, as well as the central plot. For instance, a supporting character might challenge your protagonist to temporarily overcome their flaw, which enables the protagonist to solve a problem that advances the central plot.

STEP #3: Decide whether you need an overarching plot

For those writing a trilogy or series, consider including an overarching plot that creates a sense of long-term cohesiveness. To pull this off, think about the big-picture goals of your protagonist and antagonist. What large-scale "war" are they trying to win? Then decide how each central plot in the series creates progress within the greater overarching struggle.

CONFLICT: FUELING THE PLOT FIRE

Conflict is a struggle between opposing sides. If two guys want the last slice of pizza, there will be conflict. If two parents disagree on how to raise their child, there will be conflict. If two kingdoms lay claim to a strip of land, there will be conflict. These scenarios force characters to act, and their actions become the plot.

It might help to think of plot as fire and conflict as fuel. The longer we want our plot to blaze, the more conflict we need to pour on. If we're writing a short story, we might be content with flames that turn to smoke after ten pages. However, if we want something longer, we'd better stock up on fuel.

Luckily, fictional fuel is easy to come by. Once we establish conflict, it leads to more conflict. For instance, if two guys want the last slice of pizza, they might argue over who deserves it more. Then one guy insults the other, which leads to a fistfight, which leads to a broken jaw, which leads to a hospital visit, which leads to a boiling desire for vengeance, and so on.

Note that each action in the example leads to a more serious action. In other words, the stakes are continuously raised. At first, all that's at stake is a slice of pizza, but soon pride, health, and justice are on the line. As the stakes climb higher, the story becomes more intriguing.

When creating **stakes**, we want to make sure our character has something to gain AND something to lose. Gotta have both. Many writers only give a character something to gain, and that's not enough. For example, if a gambler wants to win a poker tournament so he can earn a million-dollar prize, there's something to gain (the money). But what is there to lose? Where's the danger in failing? Why should we care if he *doesn't* get the million bucks?

To bolster the stakes, let's give our gambler a personal reason for needing the million. Say he owes a large sum of money to a ruthless crime boss, and mobsters threaten to harm his family unless he pays up. In this new scenario, he has something to gain (money) and something to lose (his family's safety). The poker tournament then takes on new meaning as it becomes a battle-ground for the fate of his loved ones.

It might help to think of gains as goals and losses as motiva-tions. In Chapter 2 we discussed how characters need goals and motivations; if we craft conflict with that in mind, stakes should arise naturally. Once the stakes are established, we can raise them by repeatedly answering the question "How can the protagonist have *even more* to lose?"

Returning to our gambler example, the story might open with loan sharks demanding money. They threaten his family, and when he fails to pay his debt, they shave his wife's head in front of him. Next time he fails, they smash up his car. From there, the threat level continually increases: they kidnap the family dog, set his house on fire, take his kid hostage, etc. Finally, the poker tournament arrives, and our gambler must win to survive.

ACTION STEPS: CREATING CONFLICT AND STAKES

STEP #1: Establish two sides of the conflict

Conflict usually involves two opposing sides, with the protago-nist representing one side while the antagonist reps the other. Though you certainly can present three or more sides, most stories boil down to two "teams" battling until one prevails.

When crafting conflict, decide which team your main charac-ters belong to. In a good-versus-evil scenario, the "good" team might consist of your protagonist and their allies while the "bad" team consists of the antagonist and some henchmen. Characters can, of course, switch allegiances when appropriate, but it helps to identify both sides upfront.

STEP #2: Balance the conflict

Conflict is only interesting if it challenges characters. This means you want your protagonist to face obstacles that require meaningful effort to overcome. If the protagonist cruises through the story without breaking a sweat, the audience has nothing to engage with. Also, avoid impossible obstacles. If the conflict is totally overwhelming—like a Little League baseball team playing against the New York Yankees—then there's no realistic solution and thus no drama.

For that reason, it's best to aim for a sweet spot where your protagonist struggles but has a legitimate chance to succeed.

STEP #3: Establish the stakes

Stakes create meaning, so figure out what your character has to gain AND lose. If they pursue a job at a prestigious law firm, they'll gain money and respect. But what if they don't get the job? What's the downside? Why should we care?

Look to create personal stakes that add meaning to the situation. For instance, maybe the protagonist has a brother working at the firm, and there's a sibling rivalry at stake. Or maybe the protagonist has long been regarded as unintelligent but now has an opportunity to prove everyone wrong.

STEP #4: Raise the stakes

Establishing stakes isn't enough. Remember to raise them throughout the story. This means increasing the magnitude of what might be gained and lost.

If a story opens with a kidnapper abducting a child and leaving a ransom note, how might we raise the stakes from there? Perhaps the kidnapper then sends a series of threatening notes, each with something that belongs to the child: first the child's hair, then fingernails, then an ear… You get the picture.

The goal is to not become complacent with the initial stakes. To keep the audience engaged, we must continually apply more pressure until the conflict is resolved.

PLOT AS AN EXTERNAL JOURNEY

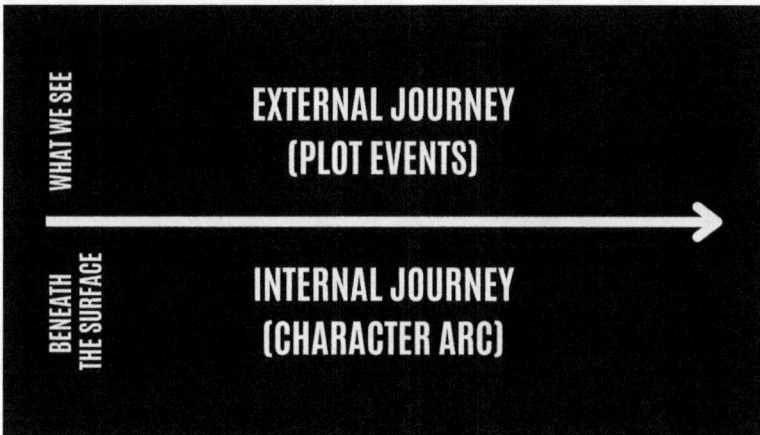

In an earlier chapter, we examined how characters undergo internal journeys. Watching characters wrestle with their flaws and lies can be cathartic, but for an internal journey to have impact, conflict must be expressed through external events.

Imagine we're writing a character who overcomes their selfishness. They start off with their flaw (selfishness) and mature toward a strength (generosity). That would make for a satisfying character arc. But how do we express this arc? Do we show the character sitting around thinking about becoming generous?

No, of course not. That would bore everyone into a coma.

Instead, dramatize the character's arc. This means revealing a series of external plot events that represent the character's internal growth. We might also surround the protagonist with other characters who represent the strength they're growing toward.

Here's a basic example. Say we introduce a self-centered mercenary named Jonathan. He's a skilled swordsman who's obsessed with money, and he needs to grow toward the strength of generosity.

Early on, someone hires him to rescue a prisoner from a band of pirates. Jonathan accepts the mission, slaughters some pirates, and locates ten hostages. However, instead of setting everyone free, he only rescues the one he was hired to find, scheming that he can demand even more money for rescuing the others. This scenario establishes his flaw (selfishness) and shows why his flaw is harmful (because innocent people suffer). It also draws a negative connection between Jonathan and the pirates—both of whom exploit the townspeople.

After he's hired to rescue the others, Jonathan visits the pirates' lair and discovers that the prisoners have been moved elsewhere. This inconvenience prompts him to return to town and demand more money (which shows him leaning harder into his flaw).

Unfortunately for him, the townspeople have learned of his schemes, and they ambush him and steal his money. If he wants it back, he must rescue the prisoners. This forces him to acknowledge the consequences of his actions and his need to change.

Desperate to reclaim his fortune, Jonathan sets out again. He encounters an escaped prisoner—a frightened young woman named Charlotte. Though he orders her to return to town for her own safety, she insists on personally rescuing the other prisoners (thus displaying the strength of generosity).

Jonathan and Charlotte then team up. When they locate the pirates' new lair, Charlotte sneaks inside to free the prisoners. Meanwhile, Jonathan waits behind, watching out for enemies. When Charlotte screams in terror, he charges in to find her surrounded by a band of blade-wielding enemies. Though outnumbered, Jonathan risks his life and intervenes in an act of self-sacrifice. The pirates chop off his sword hand, but he manages to kill his enemies and save the hostages.

Later, Jonathan awakens in bed at the town's inn. His wounded arm is bandaged, and he learns that the town doctor—Charlotte—saved him from bleeding to death. Essentially, she rewarded him for overcoming his flaw. In the end, he repays the favor by learning to fight with his other hand so he can protect her and the town. Character arc complete.

The point of this example is to illustrate how meaningful change happens outside a character's head. **Flaws, lies, and growth must be expressed through drama.** Selfishness isn't a story, but when selfishness creates suffering in a tangible world, characters can pursue internal change and external triumph.

ACTION STEPS: PLANNING AN EXTERNAL JOURNEY

STEP #1: Connect the internal to the external

Start by thinking about the internal journey. Will your character have an Upward Arc, an Outward Arc, or a Downward Arc? What flaw or lie will drive the arc? What strength or truth can the character grow toward?

Let's say you choose an Upward Arc in which the protagonist overcomes the lie that "Wealth guarantees respect." That's a good start, and it sets up for the protagonist to embrace the truth that "Wealth doesn't guarantee respect."

Next, brainstorm ways to represent that internal journey through external events. Early on, your protagonist might lose the respect of friends due to lack of money. Then, after selling his soul for a new career, he earns money but fails to earn anyone's respect. Finally, at the end, he chooses to sacrifice his lucrative career for a more fulfilling one.

STEP #2: Craft specific external events that represent internal struggles

Once you've figured out the basic external journey, it's time to get specific. Some events will naturally arise during the drafting process, but if you're failing to generate specifics, take another glance at the internal journey. Ask questions like: What lesson is the protagonist learning? What events can express that lesson? Can the story's theme provide direction?

Going back to our previous example, the protagonist believes the lie that "Wealth guarantees respect." If the thematic struggle is between wealth and respect, how can you craft events that show this?

Perhaps he takes a high-paying job and works under manipulative bosses who take credit for his ideas. Or maybe he receives a raise, and that prompts his jealous coworkers to exclude him from weekend get-togethers. Or perhaps he starts dating someone who isn't impressed with his money. Later, his date dumps him because he spends too much time at work. Such events represent the internal struggle while giving the protagonist reasons to grapple with his lie.

CHEAT SHEET

- The Three Types of Plots:
  - Overarching plots stretch across multiple entries in a series.
  - Central plots are the main focus of a given story.
  - Subplots support the central plot and often flesh out characters.
- Conflict: A struggle between two opposing sides that fuels plots.
- Plot as an External Journey: Plot events serve as an external representation of characters' internal struggles.

CHAPTER 6
STORY STRUCTURE

STRUCTURE SUPPORTS a narrative the way a skeleton supports the human body—enabling organs, muscles, and other body parts to function. If we rip away the skeleton, the body collapses into a puddle of flesh. Likewise, if we remove story structure, a narrative collapses into a clumsy pile of poorly connected events.

When I was a new writer, I never bothered to study structure —partly because I was lazy and partly because I believed that structure would suffocate my creativity. Though well-intentioned, this belief caused me to waste countless hours typing up scatterbrained novels that went nowhere. After five or six disastrous attempts, my confidence crumbled. Something needed to change. As a last resort, I bunkered down and studied structure.

Then—wouldn't you know it?—my novels started clicking. Within two years I drafted my book *Bad Parts*, won a contest called Pitch Wars, and found my swagger. Along the way, I learned that structure doesn't hinder creativity—it *enables* creativity. Audiences, whether they realize it or not, anticipate certain structural patterns. By meeting these expectations, we give them something familiar to latch onto. That familiarity anchors them in our stories and enables us to blast away with our imaginations.

With that in mind, this chapter will examine how to use structure to build meaningful stories—whether you're a writer who prefers to plan ahead or someone who discovers their story during the drafting process.

STRUCTURE: THE STORY'S SKELETON

At its most basic level, story structure has three steps: a beginning, middle, and end. **The beginning introduces the situation, the middle develops the situation, and the ending provides resolution.** These three steps apply to stories of any length, whether we're writing flash fiction or an epic seven-book series. Beginning, middle, and end are all we need to create structure and meaning. Simple, right?

Well, not for everyone. Unfortunately, when most of us try writing anything longer than a few pages, we hit rough patches where we wonder "What's supposed to happen next?" or "Why are my ideas running out of steam?" These questions haunt many creative minds.

The easiest way to answer them is to embrace a structural framework and use it to guide the story toward its conclusion. Some writers are lucky enough to internalize structure on their own; they consume tons of stories and naturally understand structure. For the rest of us, however, structure doesn't come so easily. We might be comfortable starting our story, but the middle looms ahead like a fog-covered forest. At first, the prospect of entering this mysterious area excites us, but before long we wander in circles, uncertain whether we're blazing a meaningful trail or just wasting time. Spoiler alert: it's usually the latter.

Rather than stumbling, lost in the narrative fog, it's best to adopt a structural pattern and build stories from it. Not only does this save time, but it gives audiences something familiar to grapple with.

THREE-ACT STRUCTURE AND OTHER POPULAR FRAMEWORKS

One of the most well-known structural models is the Three-Act Structure, popularized by Syd Field in his 1979 book *Screenplay: The Foundations of Screenwriting*. Field breaks down a story into three sections, or "acts." **Act 1** represents the first 25 percent of a story, in which the characters and plot are introduced. **Act 2** represents the middle 50 percent, where the protagonist steps outside their comfort zone to solve a problem. Finally, **Act 3** represents the last 25 percent, where the protagonist confronts the antagonist and decides the outcome of the story.

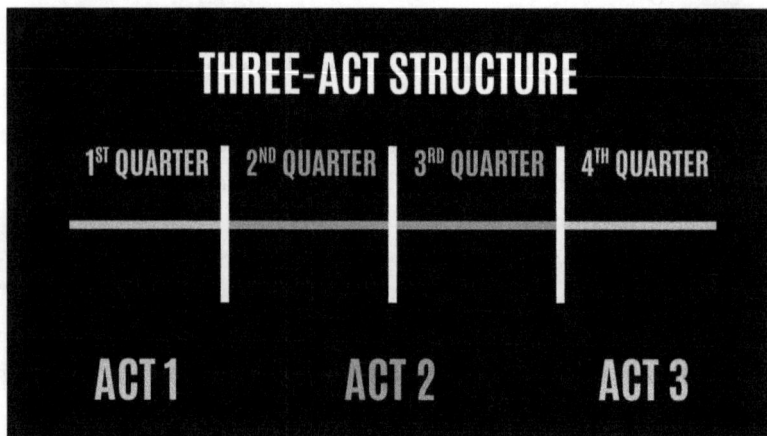

THREE-ACT STRUCTURE

| 1ST QUARTER | 2ND QUARTER | 3RD QUARTER | 4TH QUARTER |

ACT 1   **ACT 2**   **ACT 3**

Three-Act Structure provides a big-picture breakdown, but to flesh out the story and avoid the dreaded question "What's supposed to happen next?", it helps to map out several structural checkpoints. These allow for both long-term planning and short-term guidance.

Plenty of writing gurus and guidebooks offer lists of checkpoints. Some popular ones include Dan Harmon's Story Circle (8 checkpoints), the Hero's Journey (12 checkpoints), *Save the Cat's*

Beatsheet (15 checkpoints), John Truby's *Anatomy of Story* Steps (22 checkpoints), and the 27 Chapter Method. Depending on the type of writer you are, you may want to test out various structural models to see which offers the most comfort and creative freedom.

Here I'll list ten specific checkpoints that are spread across the story map. I call them the Ten Targets because this framework targets important story developments while allowing for flexibility. Remember, these are guidelines; while it helps to aim for them, it's not necessary that we hit a bullseye every time. For instance, if we aim for the Midpoint at the 50 percent mark but our actual Midpoint occurs at the 55 percent mark, we're still hitting the target board and maintaining good structure.

THE TEN TARGETS

Though often referred to as "plot structure," story structure involves more than just plot events—it also involves the main character's arc. In Chapter 2 we discussed an arc as a personal journey of transformation. Then Chapter 4 discussed how plot events are the external representation of that inner journey. This means that if we're structuring a story, we're structuring it on two levels—plot and character level.

For that reason, the Ten Targets will examine what should happen at each checkpoint for both the plot and the main character's arc. To illustrate how each checkpoint works, I'm including examples from three popular movies:

- In *Spider-Man (2002)*, Peter Parker undergoes an Upward Arc. Peter initially believes the lie "I don't need to be responsible," but after gaining spider powers and making irresponsible choices, he embraces the truth that he must be responsible.
- In *Star Wars: Episode VI - Return of the Jedi (1983)*, Luke Skywalker undergoes an Outward Arc. He believes

that the peaceful way of the Jedi will save the galaxy, and he must convince his father Darth Vader to abandon the sinister ways of the Dark Side.

- In *The Godfather (1972)*, Michael Corleone undergoes a Downward Arc. He initially holds the positive belief that he's not a criminal like the rest of his family, but after his father is shot, Michael enters the world of organized crime and soon becomes the ruthless head of the family business.

TARGET #1: OPENING HOOK
Plot Purpose: Set the story in motion and create intrigue
Character Arc Purpose: Introduce the protagonist's belief
Bullseye: 1% Mark (Beginning of Act 1)

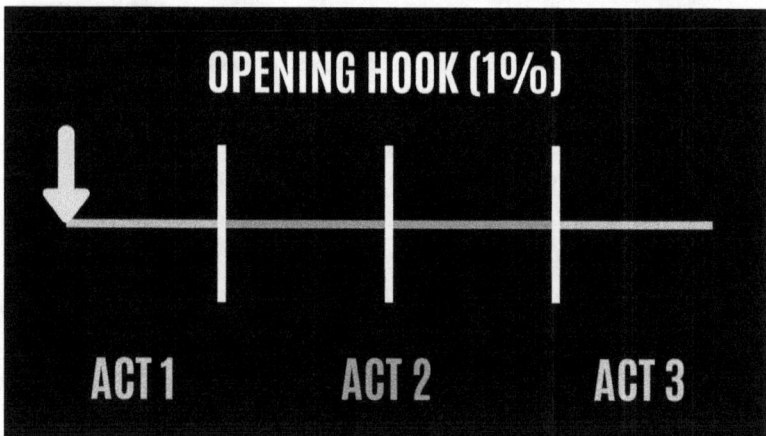

OPENING HOOK (1%)

ACT 1   ACT 2   ACT 3

The Opening Hook gets us invested. It presents something mysterious, emotional, or dramatic that seizes our attention and makes us anticipate what's to come. A hook can be as simple as hinting at someone's personal desires or as complex as a fleshed-out event in which characters overcome obstacles while pursuing a goal.

A story's genre often dictates how to hook an audience. For

instance, mysteries and thrillers hook audiences with crime and danger; horror hooks with fear and death; sci-fi and fantasy hook with technology, magic, otherworldly creatures, etc.

The most reliable hook is a strong character introduction. Unleashing a cunning villain or a compelling hero always scores points with audiences, and this is the perfect time to show a character doing what they do best, whether it's solving crimes, racing cars, or making sacrifices for loved ones. It's also a great opportunity to establish the protagonist's belief while hinting at their possibility for change.

Examples:

- *Spider-Man* (Upward Arc): The movie opens when Peter Parker is late to catch a school bus. His lateness hints at his lie ("I don't need to be responsible") and leads to two emotional hooks. First, Peter locks eyes with his love interest Mary Jane, and then he is bullied by his classmates, which creates sympathy.
- *Return of the Jedi* (Outward Arc): The final entry in the original *Star Wars* Trilogy opens with Darth Vader urging his men to finish building the second Death Star. This hook establishes a significant threat to Luke Skywalker while also reasserting Darth Vader's belief in the Dark Side of the Force.
- *The Godfather* (Downward Arc): This iconic crime drama opens by introducing the powerful mafia boss Don Vito Corleone, who agrees to deliver violent justice in exchange for a friend's loyalty. This hooks us with a glimpse into the criminal underworld while also establishing the family that protagonist Michael Corleone believes himself to be separate from.

TARGET #2: INCITING INCIDENT
  Plot Purpose: Draw the protagonist into the main conflict
  Character Arc Purpose: Challenge the protagonist's belief
  Bullseye: 12% Mark (Midway through Act 1)

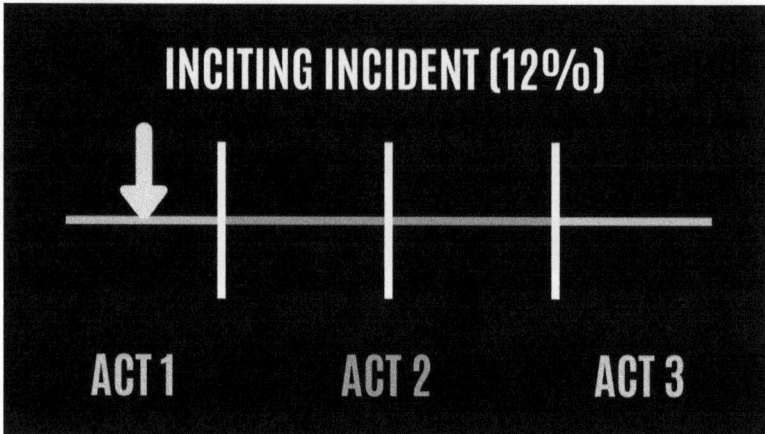

INCITING INCIDENT (12%)

ACT 1   ACT 2   ACT 3

The Inciting Incident is the event that disrupts your protago-nist's everyday life and kicks off the main conflict. The event can be a devastating, high-impact moment, like a murder that sets up a revenge story, or it can be something softer, like a couple's first meeting in a rom com.

Author K.M. Weiland claims that the Inciting Incident should raise a question that won't be answered until the story's climax. The question usually boils down to "Will the protagonist accom-plish their goal?", and the climax delivers a simple "Yes" or "No" answer. Crafting the right incident is critical—it must initiate a question that sustains the entire story.

Until this event occurs, the protagonist follows their "nor-mal" routine at work, home, etc., pursuing everyday goals. But once their world has been shaken up, the protagonist must acknowledge the main conflict. They don't necessarily *engage with* the main conflict just yet—in fact, they usually refuse to get involved—but the "door to change" is now open.

The antagonist often causes this event, either directly or indirectly. In direct cases, the antagonist personally shakes up the protagonist's life. In indirect cases, the antagonist takes action, and the consequences ripple outward until they impact the protagonist.

In terms of character arcs, this checkpoint challenges the protagonist's belief. Early on, they cling to their belief, but this event forces them to acknowledge the possibility of changing.

Examples:

- *Spider-Man* (Upward Arc): Peter is bitten by a genetically modified spider and gains superpowers. His spider abilities force him to confront his belief about responsibility.
- *Return of the Jedi* (Outward Arc): Master Yoda urges Luke to confront Darth Vader and put his Jedi beliefs to the test.
- *The Godfather* (Downward Arc): Don Vito Corleone is shot in the streets by his enemies, tempting Michael to seek revenge and protect his family. Note that this event happens about forty-two minutes into a three-hour-long movie—around the 23 percent mark. It happens later than usual because the story does plenty of legwork in establishing numerous characters and the mafia world.

TARGET #3: THE FIRST DOORWAY

Plot Purpose: Protagonist responds to the Inciting Incident, thereby engaging with the main conflict

Character Arc Purpose: Protagonist leaves their Normal World for an Upside-Down World that challenges their belief

Bullseye: 25% Mark (End of Act 1)

THE FIRST DOORWAY (25%)

ACT 1   ACT 2   ACT 3

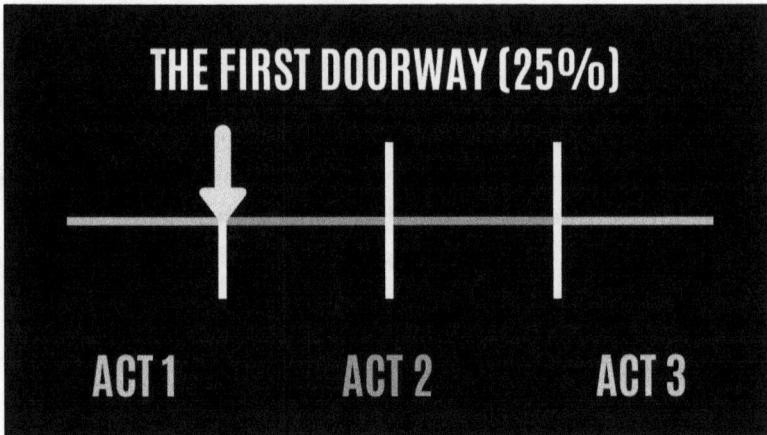

At the end of Act 1, the protagonist chooses to fully engage with the main conflict. Choice is significant here. The protagonist might decide to go on an adventure, start a new job, hunt down an enemy, run from a monster, etc. Though the protagonist doesn't choose the Inciting Incident, they do choose how they respond to it.

This is also the moment when the protagonist exits the **Normal World of Act 1** and enters the **Upside-Down World of Act 2**. This usually means a new location, but not always. For instance, the movie *Alien* takes place almost entirely aboard a spaceship. At first the ship exists as a harmless Normal World, but it becomes an Upside-Down World when the crew brings a dangerous creature aboard.

When factoring in a character arc, it's important to ask the question "How does this new world or situation challenge the protagonist's belief?" This is a great opportunity to pressure your protagonist with fresh people and obstacles that directly oppose their belief.

Examples:

- *Spider-Man* (Upward Arc): After experimenting with his superpowers, Peter chooses to use them for personal gain. Hoping to make enough money to impress his love interest Mary Jane, he participates in an underground wrestling match.
- *Return of the Jedi* (Outward Arc): Luke chooses to embark on a mission to destroy the Death Star's shield generator. His Upside-Down World will challenge his belief in the Jedi way, particularly when he later encounters Darth Vader.
- *The Godfather* (Downward Arc): Michael Corleone visits his father in the hospital and learns that the police have sent away his bodyguards. Michael chooses to pose as a mobster to prevent another assassination attempt. He later accuses police captain McCluskey of being paid off by a rival mobster. McCluskey then breaks Michael's jaw—which serves as a rite of passage when Michael then enters the world of organized crime.

TARGET #4: PINCH POINT 1

Plot Purpose: Reassert the antagonist and create problems for the protagonist

Character Arc Purpose: Antagonist punishes the protagonist for their belief

Bullseye: 38% Mark (Midway through the second quarter of the story)

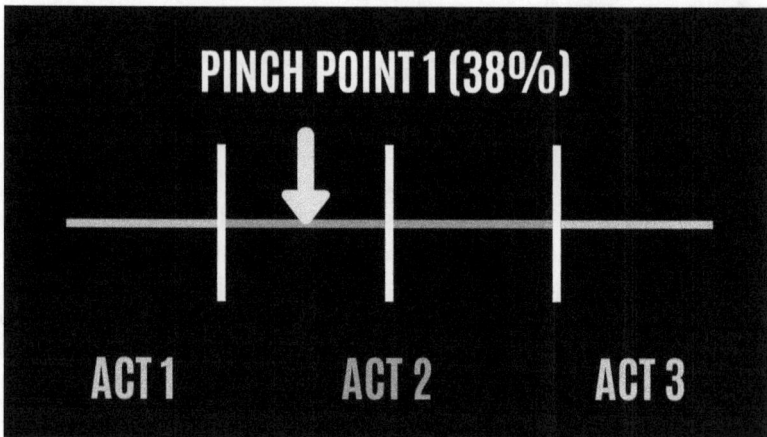

PINCH POINT 1 (38%)

ACT 1   ACT 2   ACT 3

Pinch Points are moments when an antagonist impacts the story by causing headaches for your main character. This keeps the central conflict alive while challenging the protagonist to grow.

Once Act 2 gets rolling, we need to ask "What is the antagonist up to right now?" Remember, the antagonist should be actively pursuing their own goals and creating (or at least planning to create) new obstacles for the protagonist.

In some cases, an antagonist may directly interfere with the protagonist here. Other times, the antagonist may achieve newfound power and hint at harming the protagonist in the future.

Examples:

- *Spider-Man* (Upward Arc): After being cheated out of his wrestling money, Peter refuses to stop a criminal who robs the event organizer. That same criminal kills Peter's Uncle Ben during a carjacking—thus punishing Peter for refusing to act responsibly.
- *Return of the Jedi* (Outward Arc): Emperor Palpatine

sets a trap for the Rebel Alliance, which will pay off later and challenge Luke's Jedi beliefs.

- *The Godfather* (Downward Arc): Rival mobster Sollozzo and police captain McCluskey request to meet with Michael in hopes of cooling down recent tensions between Sollozzo's people and the Corleone family.

TARGET #5: MIDPOINT

Plot Purpose: Steer the story in a new direction, usually after the protagonist learns critical new information

Character Arc Purpose: Protagonist's belief comes into conflict with its opposite, forcing the character to face the question "Who am I?"

Bullseye: 50% Mark (Middle of Act 2)

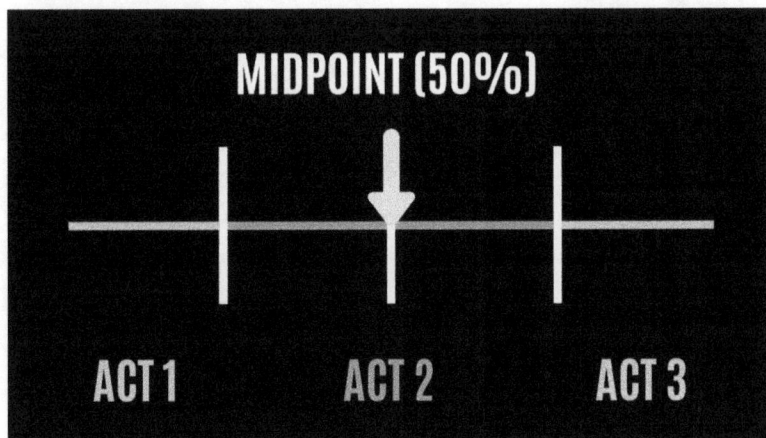

The Midpoint is a pivotal checkpoint when things shift dramatically. The protagonist—who has been reacting throughout the first half of the story—now becomes proactive. In other words, they go on the attack. Instead of playing the antagonist's game, the protagonist pursues their own solution to the main conflict.

Usually a new piece of information prompts this shift. The

protagonist may learn something about themselves, the antagonist, or the story world. Often there's a revelation, and this revelation can serve as a plot twist.

In his book *Into the Woods*, John Yorke refers to the Midpoint as a moment when "Protagonists are given a powerful 'drug' but not the knowledge to use it properly." In other words, the Midpoint changes how the protagonist perceives themselves and their situation. But it's not a cheat code. They must still go on the attack, make new mistakes, and earn victory.

When it comes to character arcs, the Midpoint forces the protagonist to acknowledge the opposite of their belief. So, in an Upward Arc, the character still possesses their negative belief (or lie) while coming face-to-face with a positive belief (or truth). In an Outward arc, the character's truth will encounter the lie. Finally, in a Downward Arc, the character holding a truth will be tested by a lie.

Examples:

- *Spider-Man* (Upward Arc): On graduation night, Peter recognizes that his irresponsible actions caused his uncle's death. This motivates Peter to proactively fight crime as Spider-Man.
- *Return of the Jedi* (Outward Arc): Luke senses Darth Vader's presence on the forest moon Endor and leaves his friends to confront Vader.
- *The Godfather* (Downward Arc): Michael murders Sollozzo and McCluskey, taking a major step toward becoming head of his crime family.

TARGET # 6: PINCH POINT 2
Plot Purpose: Reassert the antagonist and create obstacles for the protagonist

Character Arc Purpose: Antagonist punishes the protagonist for their belief

Bullseye: 62% Mark (Halfway through the third quarter of the story)

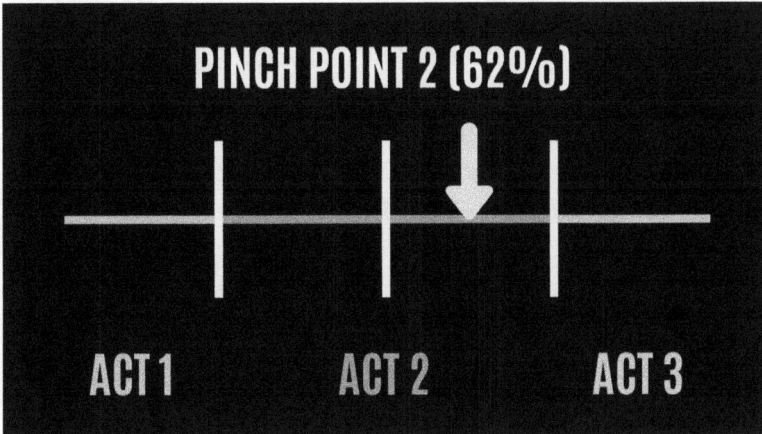

PINCH POINT 2 (62%)

ACT 1   ACT 2   ACT 3

Pinch Point 2 exists to return the antagonist to action. Since the protagonist goes on the attack after the Midpoint, it's only natural that the antagonist should counterattack. Pinch Point 2 is that counterattack. Here we raise the stakes while giving the protagonist new challenges to overcome.

Pinch Point 2 typically sets up for the protagonist's lowest moment (Target #7). This means the antagonist may set a trap or take action that makes the protagonist vulnerable.

With character arcs, consider how the Midpoint impacted the protagonist's belief. In Upward and Downward Arcs, the protagonist will be shifting toward a new belief, and at Pinch Point 2 the antagonist will punish them for this shift. In Outward Arcs, the protagonist will be punished for sticking to their belief.

Examples:

- *Spider-Man* (Upward Arc): The Green Goblin captures Spider-Man and proposes an alliance, threatening to cause city-wide harm if Spidey refuses him.
- *Return of the Jedi* (Outward Arc): Darth Vader considers returning to the Light Side but insists it's too late to change. He delivers Luke to Emperor Palpatine, who will test Luke's belief in the Jedi way.
- *The Godfather* (Downward Arc): While Michael hides overseas in Italy, his first wife is killed during an assassination attempt and his brother Sonny is murdered back in the United States. These events punish Michael for his Midpoint murders, while also paving the way for him to become head of his crime family.

TARGET #7: LOWEST LOW
Plot Purpose: Protagonist suffers a brutal setback
Character Arc Purpose: Protagonist reconsiders their belief
Bullseye: 70% Mark (Just before the end of Act 2)

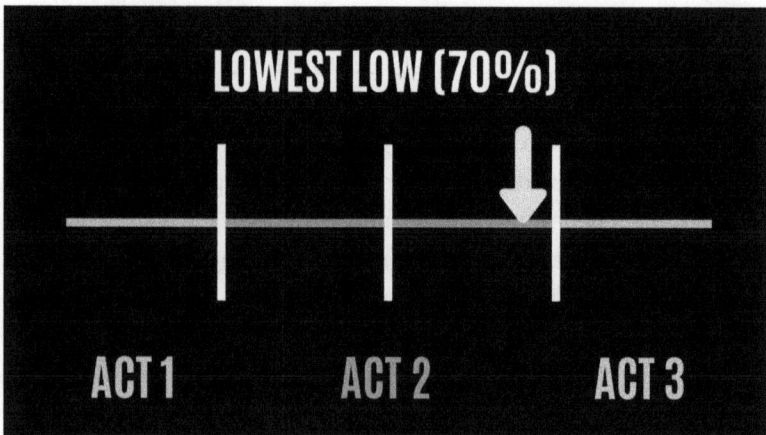

Before exiting the Upside-Down World of Act 2, the protagonist will suffer a major defeat. It often involves the death of a supporting character, the destruction of a valuable relationship, the loss of a critical item, or another devastating setback. This moment forces the protagonist to reflect on their situation before rising to the challenge in Act 3.

This is a critical moment for character arcs. In Upward Arcs, it punishes the protagonist for all the progress they've made. In Outward Arcs, it provides the greatest temptation to abandon their belief. In Downward Arcs, it creates a final push toward the negative belief.

Examples:

- *Spider-Man* (Upward Arc): The Green Goblin discovers Spider-Man's identity and attacks Peter's Aunt May.
- *Return of the Jedi* (Outward Arc): The Rebel fleet falls into the Empire's trap and sustains heavy casualties. The Emperor insists that everyone will die unless Luke joins the Dark Side.
- *The Godfather* (Downward Arc): Don Vito Corleone dies, leaving Michael alone at the head of the family, where he reigns without conscience.

TARGET # 8: THE SECOND DOORWAY

Plot Purpose: Protagonist figures out how to defeat the antagonist

Character Arc Purpose: Protagonist embraces the belief they'll carry until the story's conclusion

Bullseye: 75% Mark (End of Act 2)

THE SECOND DOORWAY (75%)

ACT 1   ACT 2   ACT 3

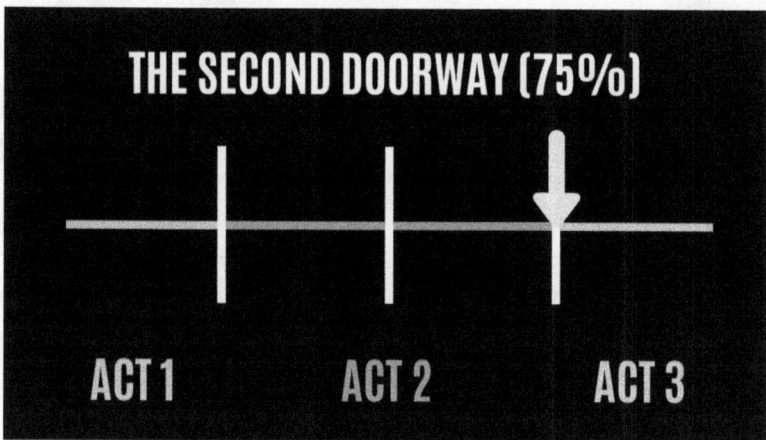

By the end of Act 2, the protagonist has survived the trip through the Upside-Down World and now yearns to confront the antagonist once and for all. But despite having overcome obstacles, made new friends, and grown as an individual, the protagonist still lacks something vital—the thing that will enable them to challenge the antagonist.

The Second Doorway is where they obtain that special something. It may be a critical piece of info, a valuable tool, or a new opportunity.

As with the First Doorway, we jump from one world to another. Earlier, we shifted from the Normal World of Act 1 to the Upside-Down World of Act 2; **as we shift into Act 3, we enter a Fusion World** that blends elements of the Normal and Upside-Down Worlds. Sometimes the protagonist will return to the Normal World with skills obtained in the Upside-Down World. Other times the protagonist will remain in the Upside-Down World and use skills from the Normal World to defeat their enemy. Ideally, we design a situation where the protagonist merges their old self and new self to resolve the central conflict.

At this stage of a character's arc, the protagonist must decide what their ultimate belief will be. They don't have to prove anything yet (because the test will come later), but they should commit to a belief and carry it into the final battle.

Examples:

- *Spider-Man* (Upward Arc): At the hospital Aunt May convinces Peter that the Goblin is attacking the people he loves most. Peter then rushes to warn Mary Jane.
- *Return of the Jedi* (Outward Arc): As the Rebel fleet continues to suffer heavy losses, Luke grabs his lightsaber in a moment of weakness and attempts to kill Emperor Palpatine. Darth Vader interferes.
- *The Godfather* (Downward Arc): With Vito Corleone dead, Michael plans to achieve power and security by assassinating the heads of rival families.

TARGET #9: FINAL BATTLE

Plot Purpose: Protagonist and antagonist battle until one side wins

Character Arc Purpose: Protagonist fully embraces their final belief

Bullseye: 88% Mark (Midway through Act 3)

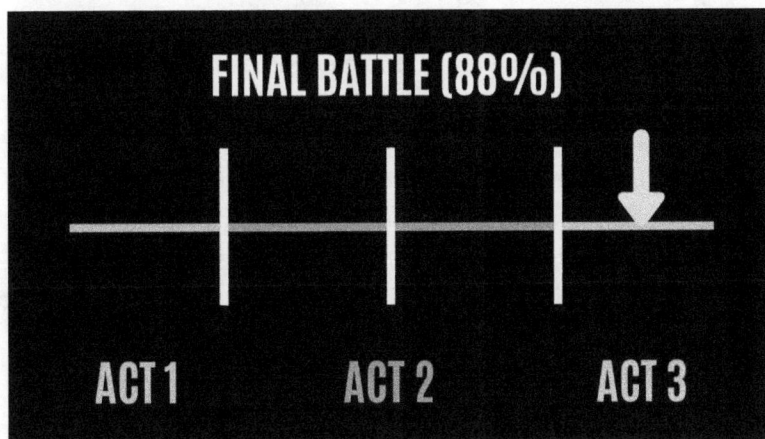

Time for the big showdown. Entering Act 3, the protagonist gathers their allies, makes last-minute preparations, and sets out for the final confrontation. Here, the story's outcome will be decided.

The Final Battle might be a literal battle, like a swordfight, or it may involve less violent conflict, like two lawyers dueling in court or two ex-lovers making up. There may also be an internal battle in which the protagonist conquers personal demons. However we choose to stage this battle, it should be difficult for the protagonist to win. Setbacks along the way will keep the audience in suspense until the protagonist makes a climactic choice.

When setting up the climactic choice, put the protagonist in a situation where they must choose between one belief and another. This dilemma should create internal conflict. Protagonists who embrace a truth will sacrifice something to achieve a greater good, while those who embrace a lie sacrifice a greater good to obtain what they desire. Either way, this choice will complete their arc and shape the story's ending.

Examples:

- *Spider-Man* (Upward Arc): Peter battles the Goblin, who reveals himself to be Norman Osborn. Osborn attempts to manipulate Peter by suggesting they have a father-son bond, but Peters declares that his real father is Uncle Ben (who represents responsibility). Osborn then launches a sneak attack but inadvertently kills himself.
- *Return of the Jedi* (Outward Arc): After defeating Darth Vader in a duel, Luke has the opportunity to kill his father, who recently threatened Leia. Instead, Luke tosses his weapon aside and chooses the nonviolent way of the Jedi. Emperor Palpatine then attempts to murder him with Force lightning, but Vader kills

Palpatine to protect his son. Luke succeeds in turning Vader back to the Light Side.

- *The Godfather* (Downward Arc): Michael eliminates his rivals and brings newfound power to the Corleone family. He then orders the murder of his abusive brother-in-law. Michael's wife Kay asks him if he had his brother-in-law killed, and Michael lies to her face. He gets what he wants—power, control, and security —while sacrificing personal relationships.

TARGET#10: ENDING

Plot Purpose: Create closure while hinting at a future for the characters

Character Arc Purpose: Show the aftermath of the protagonist embracing their new belief

Bullseye: 99% Mark (End of Act 3)

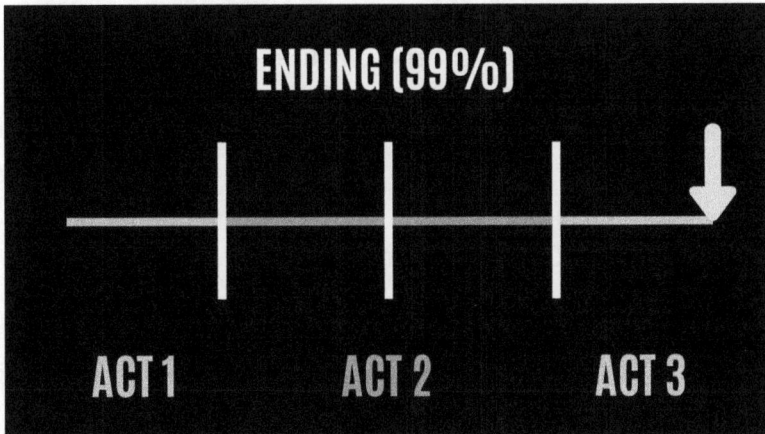

ENDING (99%)

ACT 1   ACT 2   ACT 3

The story concludes with a brief glimpse into the protagonist's life after the Final Battle. Now's the time to tie up loose ends while implying how the future will play out.

This is also a golden opportunity to create "**circularity**," which means recalling ideas that were present at the beginning.

For example, we might repeat a familiar scenario from earlier, but we update the scenario to reflect how the protagonist and their world has changed. Doing so creates a "before and after" effect that brings the story full circle.

Examples:

- *Spider-Man* (Upward Arc): Mary Jane professes her love to Peter, who rejects her. He does this to protect her and fully commit himself to his uncle's words "With great power comes great responsibility."
- *Return of the Jedi* (Outward Arc): Luke says goodbye to his fatally wounded father, who commends Luke for becoming a Jedi Knight. Later, Luke and his friends celebrate their long-awaited victory over the Empire.
- *The Godfather* (Downward Arc): Michael meets with men who address him as "Don Corleone"—a callback to the opening scene in which his father Vito is identified as Don Corleone. In the movie's final image, a door is shut on Michael's wife Kay, emphasizing how Michael has become separated from his former self.

ACTION STEPS: STRUCTURING YOUR STORY

STEP #1: Determine your main character's arc

Most stories are shaped by the protagonist, so decide upfront whether yours will undergo an Upward, Outward, or Downward Arc. Figure out what flaw or lie they'll grapple with, then determine the outcome of their journey. Determining this arc from the get-go creates a strong structural foundation to build the story upon.

STEP #2: Brainstorm the big picture

Every story needs a beginning, middle, and end.

First, think about your protagonist's Normal World. What makes it "normal" for them? How does everyday life both comfort and frustrate them? What could potentially shake up their life?

Next, consider how your protagonist shifts from their Normal World to an Upside-Down World. Sometimes this means visiting a new location. Other times, the Normal World is stricken with harsh changes, like terrorists taking over an office building or ghosts haunting a small town. Either way, once the protagonist reaches the Upside-Down World, they meet new people and face new challenges. Both should influence the protagonist and push them toward change.

Finally, consider the Fusion World. How can your protagonist combine their original self and new self to resolve the main conflict? In other words, how does your protagonist both stay the same AND change? Maybe they use old skills with a new approach, or maybe they share new knowledge with old friends.

STEP #3: Aim for the Ten Targets

Create a list of the Ten Targets and brainstorm whatever ideas come to you. Don't worry about getting everything perfect. For now, let the ideas flow. You don't have to complete the Targets in order—work on whichever excites you most. If you love your Ending, write about it and work backward. If you have a clever idea for a Midpoint, build around that.

If you're not sure where to begin, try this:

Start with the Inciting Incident—it proposes your story's main question, which must be answered during the Final Battle.

Once you determine the central question and answer, the other Targets become easier to hit. For example, if the question is "Will the hero save his office building from terrorists?" the answer will either be "Yes" or "No." If you pick "Yes," then you must write a Midpoint that sends your protagonist toward that "Yes" outcome. From there, the Doorways, Pinch Points, and Lowest Low should fall into place. Then all that's left is figuring out a compelling Hook and a satisfying Ending.

Structuring a story doesn't mean nailing down every single detail from the get-go. Rather, create broad strokes that offer direction. Later, when you start drafting, the finer details emerge. Those details often change the story's direction, and when that happens, there's no need to panic. Creativity is chaos, after all, and a strong story is one that strikes a balance between chaos and order.

So allow creativity to take you on an adventure. And if you become hopelessly lost in the fog, let structure be your guide as you discover your way through one scene at a time.

Speaking of scenes, get ready to tackle them in our next chapter.

CHEAT SHEET

- Story Structure includes a beginning, middle, and end.
- Story Structure combines both plot structure and character arcs. These create a narrative that is engaging on both external (plot) and internal (character) levels.
- The Ten Targets include:

1. Opening Hook: Sets the story in motion; introduces the protagonist's belief.
2. Inciting Incident: Draws protagonist into the main conflict; forces protagonist to question their belief.
3. The First Doorway: Protagonist chooses to enter the Upside-Down World; their belief is challenged here.
4. Pinch Point 1: Antagonist creates problems; punishes the protagonist for their belief.
5. Midpoint: New info compels the protagonist to become proactive; the protagonist's belief faces its opposite.
6. Pinch Point 2: Antagonist creates more problems, further punishes the protagonist for their belief.
7. Lowest Low: Protagonist suffers a major defeat, must reconsider their belief.
8. The Second Doorway: New info enables the protagonist to confront the antagonist; protagonist chooses their final belief.
9. Final Battle: Decides the story's outcome; the protagonist embraces their belief with a climactic choice.
10. Ending: Ties up loose ends and hints at a future, shows the outcome of the character embracing their final belief.

CHAPTER 7
SCENES

REMEMBER in the previous chapter when we talked about structure being the story's skeleton? Now we're gonna zero in on scenes—which function like the individual bones within the skeleton. Scenes not only support the overall structure, but they also bring characters, themes, and plot events to life.

In fact, scenes *are* life. Each scene—whether major or minor, long or short, suspenseful or calm—creates a fictional reality by transforming raw ideas into concrete moments. Those moments generate emotion, and if we hope to satisfy an audience, we need to keep the emotion flowing from the opening scene to the final one.

This chapter will focus on crafting powerful scenes. We'll look at how they're designed, how they create meaningful change, and how they enrich the overall story.

SCENE STRUCTURE: BUILDING THE TWO TYPES OF SCENES

We already described scenes as the bones of a story, but the technical definition of a scene is a **structured storytelling unit in which something changes**. Structure is especially critical because without it, scenes lack focus and purpose.

In his book *Techniques of the Selling Writer*, Dwight V. Swain outlined two basic types of scenes, which he labeled "Scenes" and "Sequels." His terminology can be confusing, so for clarity's sake, we'll call them "Action Scenes" and "Reaction Scenes." Here we'll define both types and the three-step pattern for building them.

TYPES OF SCENES

ACTION SCENE	REACTION SCENE
• GOAL	• REACTION
• CONFLICT	• DILEMMA
• RESOLUTION	• DECISION

ACTION SCENES
STAGE 1: GOAL
STAGE 2: CONFLICT
STAGE 3: RESOLUTION (USUALLY DISASTER)

In an Action Scene, a character pursues a **GOAL**. The scene goal can be as lofty as world domination or as mundane as taking allergy medicine, but the character must pursue something. A detective might pursue evidence, a fugitive might pursue a safe haven, a teenager might pursue a prom date, an athlete might pursue a bottle of Gatorade—you get the idea.

While chasing their goal, the character faces **CONFLICT**, or obstacles that prevent them from achieving the goal. Obstacles come in many forms—everything from human opponents to dangerous terrain to personal fears.

After characters overcome obstacles, the scene reaches its **RESOLUTION**. Sometimes the resolution is triumphant, and the character achieves their goal without creating new problems. However, in most cases, Action Scenes end in **DISASTER**, meaning the character either falls short of the goal or they achieve the goal while suffering an unexpected setback. We typically want disastrous outcomes because they lead to compelling Reaction Scenes, which brings up our next type.

REACTION SCENES
STAGE 1: REACTION
STAGE 2: DILEMMA
STAGE 3: DECISION

The outcome of an Action Scene should prompt **EMOTIONAL REACTIONS** from characters. Note that "emotional" doesn't necessarily mean over-the-top or melodramatic. Characters *can* cry their eyes out if warranted, but usually we want subtle reactions like frustration, embarrassment, or discouragement.

Following their reaction, the character faces a **DILEMMA**. They ask themselves, "What can I do now? What are my options? What course of action should I take?" Dilemmas force a character to consider two equally unappealing options. Internal conflict results when the character struggles to choose between them—a clever character may even conjure an unexpected third option.

After the dilemma stage, our character makes a **DECISION** and chooses to pursue a new goal. This prompts another Action Scene, which leads to another Reaction Scene, and so on.

To better illustrate how Action and Reaction Scenes work, let's look at examples. We'll start with the interrogation scene from *The Dark Knight*. This iconic Action Scene occurs after

Batman captures the Joker and takes him to the police station. Here are the scene's three phases:

- GOAL: Batman wants the locations of Harvey Dent and Rachel Dawes.
- CONFLICT: Batman struggles to intimidate the Joker into revealing their locations.
- DISASTER: The Joker reveals that Harvey and Rachel are in separate locations and that Batman only has enough time to rescue one person.

This is followed by a brief Reaction Scene:

- REACTION: Batman slams the Joker to the ground in frustration.
- DILEMMA: Lieutenant Gordon asks whether Batman will help Harvey or Rachel.
- DECISION: Batman decides to pursue Rachel, his new goal.

Note that the Reaction Scene is much shorter than the preceding Action Scene. Sometimes the situation dictates that a character must make a quick decision. In this case, Batman can't stand around weighing his options, so he (and the Reaction Scene) must hurry.

For another example, *Raiders of the Lost Ark* opens with Indiana Jones navigating the jungles of Peru in pursuit of treasure. Initially we get an Action Scene:

- GOAL: Indy wants treasure that's hidden inside a temple.
- CONFLICT: Deadly traps threaten him.
- DISASTER: He obtains the golden idol, but removing it causes the temple to collapse.

This disaster prompts a brief Reaction Scene:

- REACTION: Indy fears for his life.
- DILEMMA: Should he return the idol to its pedestal or run away?
- DECISION: Indy runs for his life.

His decision leads to a new goal and another Action Scene:

- GOAL: Escape the tomb.
- CONFLICT: Indy encounters more traps, and his partner betrays him.
- DISASTER: After narrowly escaping with the golden idol, Indy encounters his rival Belloq, who steals the treasure. Indy finds himself surrounded by a group of hostile enemies who are loyal to Belloq.

This leads to—you guessed it—another Reaction Scene:

- REACTION: Indy is frustrated by the turn of events.
- DILEMMA: Recover the idol? Or flee the area?
- DECISION: Indy runs to board an airplane.

ACTION STEPS: STRUCTURING YOUR SCENES

STEP #1: Identify the type of scene you're working with

Whether you're planning out an unwritten scene or revising an existing one, it's important to identify whether you're crafting an Action or Reaction Scene. The easiest way to distinguish between them is to recognize which type of conflict is present. If characters face external conflict from physical obstacles and opponents, it's an Action Scene. If characters face internal conflict in the form of a dilemma, it's a Reaction Scene.

STEP #2: Ensure that the scene has three stages

Action scenes follow a Goal-Conflict-Resolution pattern and usually end in disaster. To create impactful Action Scenes, build toward an unexpected disaster. If a character achieves their goal, make something go wrong—or at least hint that something will turn rotten in the future. For example, if a man asks a woman to marry him and she says "Yes," that "Yes" might come with a hesitance that foreshadows future complications.

Reaction scenes, meanwhile, follow the pattern Reaction-Dilemma-Decision. The key to making these interesting is to highlight the emotion, then delve into the dilemma. Audiences love balanced dilemmas, so have your character weigh two bad options. These scenes can be especially engaging if the character becomes strategic or seeks advice from trusted friends.

STEP #3: String together Action and Reaction Scenes

Stories follow a pattern of cause and effect: something happens, which causes something else to happen, which causes *something else* to happen, and so on. Action and Reaction Scenes make this cause-and-effect pattern possible. When an Action Scene ends in disaster, characters must react, and the ensuing Reaction Scene leads to a decision, which necessitates another Action Scene.

Some writers fear their stories will grow repetitive or predictable if everything is Action, Reaction, Action, Reaction, etc. That's a valid concern, and one way to shake things up is to create different plot lines to keep the audience guessing.

For example, pretend we're writing a teen romance with two plot lines. The first involves the protagonist Sara trying to attract a classmate named Kevin. The second involves Sara trying to earn a starting role on the varsity soccer team.

Let's say we open with an Action Scene in which Sara wants to coax Kevin into asking her to the prom (Goal). She flirts with him, but the conversation becomes awkward (Conflict). Still, she persists, and—uh-oh—Kevin reveals that he's planning to ask out her best friend Amy (Disaster).

Following this disaster, we build a Reaction Scene in which the humiliated Sara runs into the bathroom to collect herself (Reaction). Once her emotions cool down, she faces a dilemma: she can accept the heartbreak, or she can sabotage Kevin's plan to ask out Amy. Ultimately, Sara's decision is to ruin Amy's reputation.

We can continue with this romantic plot, but if we do, the story might feel simplistic. Instead, let's switch to the soccer plot. Not only does this keep the story fresh, but it also builds suspense by making the audience wait for the outcome of the romantic plot.

In the next Action Scene, Sara practices hard to impress her soccer coach (Goal). Unfortunately, however, Sara is challenged throughout practice by the older girls (Conflict), and she sprains her ankle after running into a teammate (Disaster).

This disaster is followed by a Reaction Scene in which she lies in bed frustrated and unable to walk (Reaction). She faces a dilemma about how to get healthy in time for her next soccer game: she can either rest her ankle or ask her drug-dealing older brother for painkillers. She decides to contact him tomorrow. Right now, however, she wants to damage Amy's reputation on social media, which means we jump back to the romantic plot with a new Action Scene.

SCENE VALUES: CREATING MEANINGFUL CHANGE

Earlier we established that a scene is a structured unit of storytelling in which something *changes*. Here we'll focus on making those changes happen by using what are called scene values. First popularized by screenwriting guru Robert McKee, a **scene value** is something that's at stake in a given scene: information, emotion, status, power, etc. At the beginning of a scene, the value at stake will have a "charge" that is either positive or negative. By the end of the scene, the charge should shift to its opposite.

For example, if a detective wants to determine how a victim was murdered, the value at stake would be KNOWLEDGE. Its charge would initially be negative because the detective hasn't found any clues. But if our detective discovers the murder weapon, the value shifts from negative (Ignorance) to positive (Knowledge).

Here's another example. Say a fugitive has escaped from prison. At the beginning of the scene, the value at stake is FREEDOM, and it's positive because the fugitive is currently free. But if our fugitive is caught by the police, that value shifts from positive (Free) to negative (Captured).

In an **efficient scene**, at least one value changes. If nothing changes, the story remains stuck in neutral. For that reason, it helps to examine completed scenes and determine whether meaningful change is present. If it isn't, consider revising that scene by selecting a value and shifting its charge either positively or negatively.

If you're struggling to come up with a value shift, consider the following pairs of opposites:

- Love/hate
- Health/sickness
- Life/death
- Knowledge/ignorance
- Belief/cynicism
- Truth/deception
- Hope/despair
- Courage/cowardice

- Self-awareness / self-deception
- Order / chaos
- Possession / loss
- Understanding / confusion
- Safety / danger
- Self-preservation / self-sacrifice

SCENE VALUES

POSITIVE CHANGE

$$\ominus \rightarrow \oplus$$

IGNORANCE	KNOWLEDGE
DANGER	SAFETY
COWARDICE	COURAGE

NEGATIVE CHANGE

$$\oplus \rightarrow \ominus$$

LIFE	DEATH
HOPE	DESPAIR
BELIEF	CYNICISM

Now let's revisit the interrogation scene from *The Dark Knight*, this time with scene values in mind. When Batman interrogates the Joker, the value at stake is KNOWLEDGE, specifically the knowledge of Harvey and Rachel's locations. At first, the value is negative because Batman doesn't possess this info. However, once the Joker provides their locations, the value shifts from negative (Ignorance) to positive (Knowledge).

Next is the brief Reaction Scene in which Batman has to choose which hostage to pursue. The value at stake is CONTROL OF THE SITUATION, and it starts with a negative charge since Batman hasn't made a decision. However, once Batman decides to help Rachel, the charge shifts from negative (Lack of Control) to positive (Control).

When Indiana Jones hunts down the golden idol in *Raiders of the Lost Ark*, TREASURE is the value at stake. At first it's negatively charged because Indy doesn't possess the idol. But once he grabs it, the value shifts from negative (Lacking Treasure) to positive (Possessing Treasure).

When the tomb collapses, a short Reaction Scene follows. The value at stake is SURVIVAL. Indy decides to flee the collapsing tomb, and the value shifts from negative (Danger) to positive (Safety).

In the ensuing escape scene, the value at stake is once again TREASURE. This time it starts with a positive charge because the idol is in his possession. However, the value shifts from positive (Possessing Treasure) to negative (Lacking Treasure) when the idol is stolen by Belloq.

Note that scenes can have more than one value at stake. For example, in the climactic "I am your father" scene from *Star Wars: The Empire Strikes Back*, two values are at stake: HEALTH and INNOCENCE. Initially, Luke Skywalker is physically healthy and mercifully unaware of Darth Vader's identity. By the end of the scene, however, Luke's hand is chopped off (a negative shift from Healthy to Injured), and he learns that Darth Vader is his father (a negative shift from Innocence to Awareness). The two values shift, and they pressure Luke into making a desperate decision in the Reaction Scene that follows.

ACTION STEPS: CREATING CHANGE IN YOUR SCENES

STEP #1: Identify what value changes

Some scenes contain obvious changes: a character dies, a valuable object is stolen, a puppy is adopted, etc. Then there are scenes where the change may be more subtle: a spouse hints at becoming unfaithful, a child stops trusting a parent, a follower doubts their leader. Regardless of whether the change is obvious or subtle, make sure it happens.

STEP #2: If no values change, revise the scene

Many new writers make the mistake of creating scenes that have no short- or long-term consequences. If you spot one of these scenes in your work, cut it.

If you can't cut the scene for some reason (perhaps it includes a critical piece of exposition), include a value shift that makes the scene more efficient. Sometimes this means adding a new value; other times it means revising the scene's conflict or dilemma. Either way, look to include values that are relevant to your plot and character arcs.

STEP #3: Create a meaningful value shift

To make the most of a value shift, ensure that the shift itself is discernible, believable, and necessary.

Making it discernible doesn't mean yelling out, "Hey audience, pay attention to this value shift!" but it does mean presenting evidence of the shift. Even something as simple as a change in a character's facial expression can accomplish this.

In terms of believability, make sure the shift is reasonable within the context of the scene. If boy meets girl in contemporary America, it's reasonable for boy to obtain girl's phone number. It would be far less believable if he obtained her apartment key at this stage.

Finally, make sure the value shift is necessary. Any scene could potentially host hundreds of value changes, but we want to focus on what's important. Identify values that impact your character arcs, story themes, and plot. If a value pushes the other key elements forward, it's probably a keeper.

THEME: WHAT CHARACTERS SEEK IN EACH SCENE

There's an old saying that each scene is "the story in miniature." I forget where I first came across this advice, but it's a worthwhile reminder that any given scene should represent the greater whole. Not every scene has to be a mini-snapshot of the main conflict, but each scene should explore the story's themes—more specifically, *the characters* should explore the theme in each scene.

Earlier, we discussed how characters struggle with a lie or flaw that prevents them from being happy. The process of overcoming lies and flaws is known as a character arc, and completing these arcs involves embracing the theme. But this doesn't happen instantly. It's an ongoing process that occurs while characters pursue the theme in scene after scene.

Let's again consider *The Dark Knight*. The movie's thematic question is "How far must lawful people go to impose order on a chaotic world?" We encounter this theme constantly, with Batman seeking order while the Joker courts chaos. In the interrogation scene, Batman intimidates the Joker in hopes of restoring order across Gotham. Meanwhile, the Joker challenges Batman's beliefs about the rules that organize society. Eventually, Batman demands Harvey and Rachel's locations (which would restore order), but he receives false info about their locations (which creates chaos). This struggle between order and chaos shapes the film's scenes and provides characters with a clear thematic target to aim for.

Raiders of the Lost Ark raises the thematic question "What treasures are most valuable?" Indiana Jones constantly pursues treasure, as we see in the opening sequence when he claims the golden idol. Later, he seeks the Ark of the Covenant, but that's not the only treasure Indy pursues. Over time, he learns to cherish his ex-girlfriend Marion Ravenwood. Much like his artifacts, Marion is gained and lost on multiple occasions until he finally recognizes that her love is his real treasure. In the movie's closing scene, Indy abandons the Ark and chooses to embrace a future with Marion.

ACTION STEPS: SCENES WITH THEMES

STEP #1: Determine your story's thematic question

We discussed themes in detail in Chapter 4, but if you need a refresher, a story's theme is what creates meaning, unites the other narrative elements, and guides a character's arc. With that in mind, decide what your story's thematic question is and mark it down so you have it handy throughout the writing process.

STEP #2: Connect scenes to your theme

Theme is an excellent litmus test for determining whether a scene belongs in your story. When examining individual scenes, try drawing connections between them and your theme. If a scene doesn't connect with your theme, either cut or revise that scene. You can also save yourself time by ensuring that each plot line connects with your theme. When plot lines connect with the theme, typically the scenes within them do as well.

For example, if you're working with the theme of justice, you might explore different types of justice throughout the narrative. The main plot might involve a detective seeking to expose someone who got away with murder. There might also be a revenge subplot where the detective gets even with a backstabbing coworker. Finally, you might include a romantic subplot in which our detective dates a lawyer who has lost faith in the legal system and now seeks vigilante justice.

CHEAT SHEET

- Scene: a structured unit of storytelling in which something changes.
- Two Types of Scenes:

1. Action Scenes
   - Stage 1: Goal
   - Stage 2: Conflict
   - Stage 3: Resolution (usually Disaster)
2. Reaction Scenes
   - Stage 1: Reaction
   - Stage 2: Dilemma
   - Stage 3: Decision

- Scene Value: something at stake in a given scene—information, emotion, status, etc. At the beginning of a scene, the value will have a "charge" that is either positive or negative. By the end of the scene, the charge should shift to its opposite.
- Scenes are "the story in miniature," and characters should seek the story's theme in each scene.

CHAPTER 8
PACING

PACING IS the story's rhythm. It's how we convey the momentum, intensity, and timing of events. Any good rhythm alternates between speeds, and that's why narratives should heat up and cool down when appropriate. Although audiences may crave fast-paced thrillers or slow-burn dramas, a story can't be exclusively fast or slow. If everything is fast, nothing is fast. And if there's no variation, the audience becomes bored out of their brains.

It might help to think of pacing as a burning fuse. The moment we light it, a flash of excitement gives us something to anticipate. The length, brightness, and speed at which the fuse burns is what captivates audiences until the thrilling explosion.

Much like theme, pacing is an abstract element. We can't see it, but that doesn't diminish its importance. Pacing affects everything from the overall narrative to the moments within scenes, and when done right, it enhances the emotional journey.

This chapter will focus on both large-scale and small-scale pacing. We'll study how this element works, how emotions influence our perception of momentum, and how to use pacing-related tools to grip an audience from start to finish.

LARGE-SCALE PACING: PACING THE OVERALL STORY

We've all encountered bad pacing. Too slow, too fast, too inconsistent—when it comes to narrative speed and rhythm, these issues pop up everywhere.

Most writers fear penning something that feels agonizingly slow. After all, nobody wants to bore an audience. But how do we prevent slow pacing? One way is by ensuring that each scene serves a purpose. We want to avoid "empty" scenes that fail to push forward our characters, themes, or plots. Any aimless or redundant scenes should be cut or revised. Same goes for filler within scenes—things like repetitive character interactions, wandering dialogue, or excessive description. We'll talk more about this later in the Action Steps section.

Now, what about when the pace outruns the story? That means we're rushing through events, and it often happens when character reactions are partially or entirely skipped. For instance, picture a hospital scene where a middle-aged man receives a terminal diagnosis, then instantly selects a treatment plan—that scene would suck because we can't absorb the guy's emotional reaction or see how he wrestles with his treatment dilemma. If we don't give high-impact events room to breathe, we squander the emotion.

NARRATIVE SPEED

Regardless of whether we're crafting a lightning-fast thriller or a slow-burn romance, narrative speed should increase over time. Most stories start relatively slowly, then gradually accelerate before reaching max speed toward the end. Audiences have been conditioned to expect this pacing pattern, and writers should use it to their advantage by intensifying conflict and raising the stakes as the narrative progresses.

During a story's opening act we have the opportunity to introduce characters, scenarios, and worldbuilding details without having to hurry. This doesn't give us a free pass to unload massive info dumps, but audiences will forgive a relatively slow setup.

Once intros are squared away, the pace ramps up as the main conflict sizzles. Characters battle back and forth while overcoming obstacles, facing dilemmas, and learning new info that propels the story forward.

By the time the final confrontation arrives, most (if not all) exposition should be taken care of, which clears the table and allows the key players to decide the story's outcome. Here the conflict is fierce, the stakes are staggering, and the pace hits top speed.

Though this straightforward pacing pattern is reliable, there's certainly room for flexibility. For instance, *Star Wars: The Empire Strikes Back* opens with an intense battle sequence before shifting to a slower-paced second act that builds toward a gripping finale. This type of "Sandwich Pacing" works in *Empire* because the stakes are consistently raised throughout. When experimenting with different pacing styles, ensure that the structure is solid and the stakes keep climbing—otherwise, audiences may sense that the story peaked too soon.

Narrative Rhythm

Pacing requires rhythm, which means alternating between fast and slow sections. Regardless of the overall pace, a story's intensity must rise, fall, rise, fall, and rise again to stay fresh. Though it's tempting to keep a story exhilarating at all times, variation is critical.

Even lightning-quick movies like *The Terminator* need to ease off the gas pedal. That's why the film's thrilling action sequences give way to low-energy scenes. These **"cooldown" sections** preserve the pace while integrating quieter character moments and worldbuilding. Then the rapid-fire action resumes and lands with renewed impact.

As for slow-burn stories, without proper variation they can turn into snoozers. This doesn't mean we need to tack-on shootouts and explosions, but a slower tale can benefit from increased tension or hints at future conflict. We see this in the 1980 movie *The Shining*, which patiently establishes the Overlook Hotel's haunted history and Jack Torrence's potential to become violent toward his family. When Jack snaps at his wife or stares menacingly into space, the tension increases. These moments foreshadow his descent into madness while also creating a steady-yet-powerful rhythm that drives the movie toward its blood-soaked climax.

ACTION STEPS: PACING THE BIG PICTURE

STEP #1: Eliminate unnecessary scenes

The best time to adjust pacing is during the revision stage. Once your first draft is complete, try jotting down each scene from memory. Resist the urge to flip through your manuscript; instead, write down only the scenes you remember. Those tend to be the strongest and most important.

After assembling a list of scenes, flip through your manuscript and notice which ones you forgot about. You should consider cutting these. If they contain necessary plot details, try transplanting those details into a more important scene.

STEP #2: Give high-impact moments room to breathe

Once the excess scenes have been scrapped, identify your story's key emotional moments—highs, lows, victory, death, forgiveness, betrayal, and so on. Make sure they aren't all crammed together. If they are, space them out. You might want to add a cooldown scene or rearrange the overall sequence of events. Either way, make sure your story's most intense moments aren't smothering each other.

STEP #3: Ensure that the pace changes

A story with one speed is a story that's flatlining, so increase and decrease momentum when appropriate. Fast-paced, high-conflict sequences only work if the story contains slower periods of introspection, planning, and quiet emotion. The fast/slow balance doesn't have to be fifty-fifty, but survey your overall story and identify areas where the pace is lopsided. From there, see if you can reorder or revise scenes for variation.

STEP #4: Continuously raise the stakes

As the story progresses, characters should have more to gain and more to lose. By raising both the external (plot) and internal (character) stakes, we create a sense of progress while injecting tension. If any section of your story feels flat, apply more pressure to your protagonist. Put their external and internal goals in jeopardy.

SMALL-SCALE PACING: PACING A SCENE

Let's get our microscopes out and study the small stuff. In the previous chapter, we established that scenes are the building blocks of a story. They shape the narrative and thereby shape its pacing. So if we want to control a story's pace, we need to manage the speed of individual scenes.

The way to do this is to identify the "beats" within a scene. **Beats** are turning points that cause change. They include emotion beats (events that change how a character feels), action beats (physical actions and dialogue), and information beats (new info that causes a reaction). A scene's pacing depends on how many beats are present and how much time passes between them.

Say a scene opens with a dirty cop returning home from work. At the front door he notices an angry look in his wife's eyes (emotion beat). Something is obviously wrong, and he asks why she's upset (action beat). She responds by storming into the kitchen (action beat). He then follows her (action beat) and finds a mobster sitting at the kitchen table with a coffee mug in one hand and a loaded pistol in the other (information beat).

To alter this example's pacing, we could adjust either the number of beats or the length of time between them.

To speed things up, we could cut the early beats and open the scene with the cop entering the kitchen. If we want to retain those early beats, we might boost the pace by shortening the interactions between husband and wife.

If we want slower pacing, we could either add or flesh out details. To revise and slow things down, say the cop arrives home, attempts an unrequited kiss, and studies his anxious wife. He notices muddy footprints in the hallway, which is strange because she always insists that visitors remove their shoes upon entering. When he asks about the mud, she starts sobbing and storms into the kitchen, saying she'll never forgive him. He stands there puzzled, trying to make sense of her behavior, before entering the kitchen where the mobster awaits.

Note that "slow" doesn't mean boring. Slower scenes like the revised example allow tension to build while the audience anticipates the outcome. Adding details can intensify a scene's emotional impact—but don't go overboard. The trick is to include what's necessary while finding compelling ways to stretch the tension between beats.

Fiction writers can also control a scene's pacing by managing the length of sentences and paragraphs. Shorter sentences and paragraphs tend to speed things up.

On the other hand, longer sentences and paragraphs slow the pacing, which can create a steady rhythm that draws the reader in. However, a sentence or paragraph that drags on for an extended period of time with loads of excess verbiage and unnecessary details can test the reader's patience and disrupt the storytelling magic by drawing needless attention to the sentences and paragraphs themselves, especially in cases where the writer inflates the word count for the sake of beefing up a sentence or paragraph.

In an effort to boost this book's pace, I won't include an Action Steps section for Small-Scale Pacing. We've already covered the important strategies, and the best advice I can give about scene pacing is to experiment by adding, deleting, and rearranging beats until you hit your desired pace.

TOOLS FOR PACING: THE THREE INTELLECTUAL EMOTIONS

The easiest way to control narrative momentum is through three specific emotions: curiosity, suspense, and surprise. These intellectual emotions engage the mind by creating anticipation. When audiences anticipate an outcome, they take greater interest in the story. They feel tension. They yearn for relief. They become mesmerized by a satisfying narrative momentum.

For clarity, let's go through each of the three and how they impact a story:

CURIOSITY

This quality makes us want to learn more about something. If a stranger parks their motorcycle in the middle of a busy highway at midnight, we want to know who the person is, why they did this, what they want, and why they chose this particular highway at this particular hour. These questions send our minds racing as we anticipate answers.

Curiosity is a valuable tool because it instantly impacts the audience. When presented with an intriguing image, character, or situation, people stick around for answers. In fact, it always helps to generate curiosity when introducing new characters, locations, or objects. Things like a glowing tattoo, a forbidden section of town, or a giant red "X" painted across someone's windshield can all spur curiosity from the get-go.

We can also unleash curiosity later when revealing new aspects of an established character, location, or object. For instance, once we've established the significance of someone's glowing tattoo, we can show that character engaging in strange behavior that raises questions about their intentions, motivations, and loyalties.

Suspense

Maintaining an audience's attention means creating uncertainty about the outcome of events. That's why suspense should be a constant in our fiction. It raises the most important question: *will* something happen or *won't* it? Not knowing the story's future keeps audiences gripped.

When telling our tales, we want to raise questions like the following: Will the estranged family reunite? Will the wounded man bleed to death? Will the underdogs win the game? Will the police catch the kidnapper before he strikes again? There are countless possibilities for all intensity levels, so don't limit suspense to life-and-death situations. *Any situation* can be suspenseful if we're uncertain what will happen.

Keep in mind that suspense only works if audiences care about the characters involved, which means we must do the legwork to create sympathy, empathy, or envy as discussed in Chapter 2.

Once the audience is invested, establish an approaching threat. The more immediate the threat, the stronger the suspense. If an assassin is hours away from stabbing a beloved character, audiences will worry. If that same assassin is moments away, audiences will panic. Note that threats needn't be violent—anything that interferes with a character's goals counts as a threat.

Finally, keep the audience guessing about the outcome. Success and failure should be equally likely. Signal why both can happen, then create tension by hinting back and forth before delivering the outcome.

SURPRISE

Finally comes surprise, which means delivering the unexpected. This not only prevents the story from becoming predictable, it also introduces new developments and keeps the audience alert.

There are two types of surprises: abrupt and oncoming.

Abrupt surprises come out of nowhere, without any build-up, and they propel the story in a fresh new direction. Basic events like fender benders and unannounced visits work well here. We can also create high-impact surprises, like a grandmother's 90th birthday party being interrupted by gunfire. This surprise generates suspense as we worry about everyone's safety, and it also itches our curiosity by raising questions about who's shooting, what the shooter wants, and why they chose this particular time to act.

Oncoming surprises follow proper build-up. The story sends us in a particular direction, we anticipate an outcome, but the actual outcome shocks us out of our seats. These surprises typically involve **revelations**, which occur when critical new info comes to light, or **reversals**, which involve characters shifting in an unexpected direction, perhaps when someone commits an act of betrayal. Many plot twists result from oncoming surprises, and such twists create intense anticipation for the story's future.

PACING STRATEGIES

Now that we've examined the three intellectual emotions, let's look at two practical strategies for managing and improving our story's pace.

LIGHTING MULTIPLE FUSES

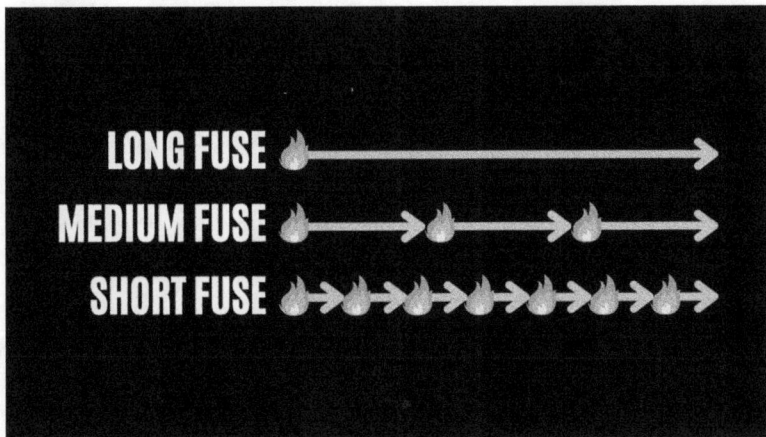

We opened this chapter by thinking of pacing as a burning fuse. Now it's time for my favorite pacing technique, a strategy called "lighting multiple fuses." Anytime we introduce a story question—big or small—we light a fuse that burns suspensefully until the question is answered. When the answer arrives, it zaps the story in a new direction.

Fuses come in different sizes. The longest ones are associated with the three types of plots discussed in Chapter 5. If we're writing a series or trilogy, the overarching plot will be our longest fuse. Next comes the central plot, which extends from a story's Inciting Incident (question) to its Final Battle (answer). Then there are subplots, which vary in length and can appear virtually anywhere. Some subplots even raise questions that span multiple entries in a series.

Medium-length fuses are associated with scenes and sequences of related scenes. For example, the opening sequence of *Raiders of the Lost Ark* raises the question "Will Indiana Jones leave Peru with the treasure?" This sequence contains multiple scenes, and each has its own fuse that generates momentum until the sequence's bigger question is answered.

Finally, short fuses. These involve scene beats. If someone throws a punch, proposes marriage, or attempts to sneak out of chemistry class, these actions pose short-term questions that juice up a scene's momentum.

To hold our audience's attention, we keep multiple fuses burning simultaneously. The shortest ones spark immediate interest while the longest glow in the background. Meanwhile, medium-length fuses create explosions of significance and unpredictability. To keep our audience engaged from start to finish, we arrange these fuses in a way that creates a healthy balance between anticipation and impact.

Weaving Different Plot Lines

Unless you're writing flash fiction, your story will likely include multiple plot lines. This is great news because alternating between two or more plot lines maintains narrative momentum.

Simply identify the major plot lines, follow one until it reaches a moment of uncertainty (a **cliffhanger**), then jump to another plot line. This strategy keeps the audience in suspense about Plot #1 while they experience Plot #2. From there, we follow Plot #2 until a moment of uncertainty, then jump back to Plot #1. Ideally, we want the nonactive plot lines to burn suspensefully in the background.

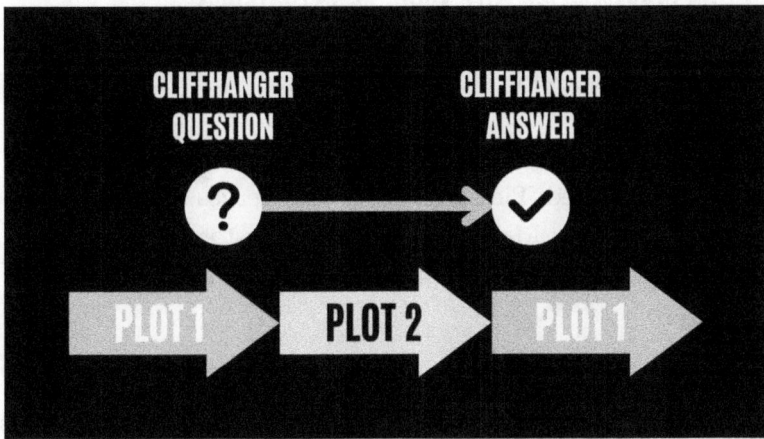

Remember the example from the previous chapter where Sara pursues her high school crush while also fighting for a starting role on the soccer team? That sequence jumps between two plot lines. Plot #1 employs a cliffhanger that raises the question "How will Sara sabotage her crush's love life?" That question creates intrigue before we switch to the soccer sequence (Plot #2), where she injures her ankle during practice. This plot uses another cliffhanger—"Will she obtain painkillers from her older brother?"—before reverting to Plot #1.

Though cliffhangers are a major component of the thriller genre, they don't necessarily need to be thrilling. Any work of fiction can benefit. Simply show conflict or a dilemma, leave the situation unresolved, and hop to another plot. Then—boom!—instant suspense.

Better yet, alternating between plot lines ensures balance, and when they overlap now and again we create a more cohesive and meaningful narrative. Best of all, when plot lines unexpectedly collide, they generate surprising outcomes that juice up the experience even more.

ACTION STEPS: PACING WITH TOOLS AND STRATEGIES

STEP #1: Choose your story's overall pace

There's no wrong answer here. Fast, medium, slow—audiences crave every speed. Pick whichever best serves your story and prepare to deliver. Make sure to keep your story's overall structure in mind and decide how breezy or intense you want the journey to be.

STEP #2: Determine how the three intellectual emotions can improve your pacing

Curiosity is the writer's best friend at the start of a story, and you'll want to rely on it during the middle stages as well. Include mysterious characters, locations, and objects. Draw inspiration from real life, and test out unexpected images to see if they create a spark.

Suspense drives a narrative and keeps the audience invested. Whether you're raising questions about who lives, who dies, or who achieves their goals, plant doubts in the audience's mind. Even if a specific outcome *has to happen* for the sake of the plot, convince the audience that it might not.

Finally, use surprise. Though too many surprises can diminish the effect, it's important to shake up a story to keep it from becoming predictable. If you're having trouble imagining a good surprise, interview your supporting characters about their darkest desires. Sometimes one selfish act can send shockwaves through a story.

STEP #3: Weave your fuses

Most stories include multiple plot lines, so weave them together in a way that keeps the audience guessing as to how each will be resolved. If your protagonist is trying to solve a murder case while also reconnecting with their estranged daughter, create opportunities for both plot lines to get a share of the spotlight— and, better yet, have them intersect at times.

As for fuses, remember that we writers are pyromaniacs— we're constantly lighting fuses of all sizes. Fire up the biggest questions early, and while those burn, ignite medium and short fuses to keep the story crackling along.

Aim to have at least one short, medium, and long fuse burning at all times—this keeps the audience concerned about the immediate present, the near future, and the overall story.

CHEAT SHEET

- Pacing is the story's rhythm. It's how the writer manages the intensity, momentum, and timing of events.
- In traditional storytelling, audiences expect most stories to begin relatively slowly. From there, the pace gradually increases, then hits max speed toward the end.
- Scene-level pacing involves adding or removing beats —or shortening or extending the number of details between beats.
- Pacing largely depends on how the writer uses three intellectual emotions: curiosity, suspense, and surprise.
- Writers can control a story's pace by raising burning questions and switching between plot lines.

CONCLUSION

THE FINAL ELEMENT

Before we wrap up, there's one final element to discuss. Though it never explicitly appears within stories, this element influences the rest. It determines which characters inhabit the fictional world. It determines how characters explore themes and drive the plot. It determines how structure, scenes, and pacing shape the narrative. Finally, it fulfills the promise of the story's concept with an unmistakable style.

The final element is the storyteller. The creative writer. The brave soul who scribbles down words in hopes of capturing the imaginations of total strangers. If you're reading this book, chances are you believe yourself to be the final element—to be part of this mysterious process we call storytelling.

Make no mistake, storytelling is a challenging and unpredictable process. There's no correct way to write a story. Strategies that work for one person may discourage the next, and writing one good story doesn't mean that the second will come easier.

What's important isn't that you write something great every time you sit at your desk—it's that you learn to adapt to each story you write. Understanding the eight key elements is a strong start. After reading this book, you should be able to unleash them in bold and creative ways.

Regardless of where you are on your personal writing journey, know that there will be good and bad writing days in your future. Both are important. Each allows you to march onward as you develop as a storyteller. So, rather than beating yourself up for the bad days, embrace them. Learn from them. Look for ways to improve. Set new goals. Experiment with new ideas.

Eventually, the bad days will give way to good ones. It will happen.

In the meantime, remember to keep on writing.

AUTHOR'S NOTE

Want to learn more about storytelling? Check out **hundreds of videos** on my YouTube channel Writer Brandon McNulty. You can also visit www.brandonmcnulty.com to request **one-on-one coaching services**.

For updates on future books, join my website's mailing list. It's a private list and your email address will never be shared with anyone. You'll also receive a free gift for signing up!

If you enjoyed this book, **please consider leaving a brief review** on Amazon, Goodreads, or wherever you purchased this book.

Finally, be sure to connect with me on social media:

youtube.com/WriterBrandonMcNulty
x.com/McNultyFiction
facebook.com/McNultyFiction
amazon.com/author/brandonmcnulty
goodreads.com/brandonmcnulty
bookbub.com/authors/brandon-mcnulty

ALSO BY BRANDON MCNULTY

Bad Parts - In "one of the most original horror novels in recent years" (Tom Deady), a career-obsessed guitarist tries to rescue her hometown from an organ-swapping demon.

Entry Wounds - In this "action-packed, surprise-filled, outrageously thrilling novel" (Jeff Strand), a high school teacher grabs a haunted gun and learns that he can't put it down—until he kills six people with it.

The Half Murders - In this "absolutely terrifying" (Felix Blackwell) novel, a mother and daughter enter a haunted house and get chopped in half by a malevolent force. For them, the nightmare is only beginning...

ACKNOWLEDGMENTS

First off, special thanks Scott Grivner for pushing me to write this book. He's one of my oldest friends (since kindergarten!), and I never considered writing a storytelling guide until he urged me to. This book doesn't happen without him.

Major thanks to everyone who critiqued the full manuscript. Samantha Zaboski and Vic Rushing delivered the early editorial punishment I needed. Mike Cucka and Meredith Funk offered eye-opening feedback and inspired me to include the "Action Steps" sections. Shell Steiner, Brandon Ketchum, Thomas Austin, Caleb Kerlin, Carol McNulty, and Denny McNulty helped me sharpen the final draft with their invaluable last-minute feedback. Sue Ducharme worked her editorial magic on every page.

Thank you to everyone who critiqued various chapters and shared valuable insights: T. Siccolinni, Kaustab Das, Tuncay Demirtepe, Felix Blackwell, Will Harwood, Maximus Carver, MethodMaster, Miles King, and Paul Miscavage.

Finally, thank you to all my YouTube supporters, whose enthusiasm for my videos has enabled me to analyze storytelling since 2019. As always, remember to keep on writing!

ABOUT THE AUTHOR

Brandon Mcnulty grew up loving monsters, demons, and the thrill of a great scare. Now he writes supernatural thrillers, horror, and other dark fiction. He is a graduate of Taos Toolbox Writers Workshop and a winner of both Pitch Wars and Revpit. He runs the popular YouTube channel Writer Brandon Mcnulty.

PRAISE FOR BRANDON MCNULTY

"*The Half Murders* is enthralling, mysterious, and absolutely terrifying. Readers beware: these twists and turns could break spines."
—Felix Blackwell, bestselling author of *Stolen Tongues*

"With his suspenseful, imaginative storytelling, Brandon McNulty is a writer to watch!"
—Jeff Menapace, author of *Bad Games*

"[*Entry Wounds* is] an action-packed, surprise-filled, outrageously thrilling novel!"
—Jeff Strand, author of *Wolf Hunt*

"*Entry Wounds* is a harrowing supernatural thriller filled with shootouts, bloodshed, betrayal—and best of all, a cursed revolver."
—Jeremy Bates, author of *Suicide Forest* and *The Sleep Experiment*

"Clever and gripping, *Entry Wounds* is a tour de force that moves as fast as the bullets from the cursed gun within its pages. You're going to want to read this ASAP."
—Robert Swartwood, *USA Today* bestselling author of *The Serial Killer's Wife*

"*Entry Wounds* makes the reader question whether, in the face of unstoppable lust for death, a predator is as tormented as his victim."
—L.C. Barlow, award-winning author of *The Jack Harper Trilogy*

"*Bad Parts* asks the intriguing question, 'What would you give up to make your body whole again? Can you put a price on your dreams?' A page-turning tale of Faustian bargains, bad choices, and hard lessons."

—Alma Katsu, author of *The Deep* and *The Hunger*

"*Bad Parts* is a non-stop thrill ride! It starts out breakneck fast and keeps accelerating—the twists keep coming tighter and darker as the novel races toward its grisly, unexpected, and thoroughly satisfying finish. "

—John Everson, Bram Stoker Award-winning author of *Covenant* and *The Devil's Equinox*

"McNulty has crafted one of the most original horror novels in recent years. [*Bad Parts*] reads like *Needful Things* if it had been written by Richard Laymon."

—Tom Deady, Bram Stoker Award-winning author of *Haven*

"*Bad Parts* gives body horror the heart replacement it needs, and this heavy metal love song about a deal with a unique kind of devil hits all the right notes as it flies by."

—Michael Arnzen, Bram Stoker Award-winning author of *Grave Markings*

"Open *Bad Parts* at your peril: you won't be putting it down until the final page is turned."

—Frederic S. Durbin, author of *A Green and Ancient Light* and *Dragonfly*